IMMORTAL DESTINY

Harold Raley

TotalRecall Publications, Inc.
1103 Middlecreek
Friendswood, TX 77546
281-992-3131 TEL
www.totalrecallpress.com

All rights reserved. Except as permitted under the United States Copyright Act of 1976, No part of this publication may be reproduced, stored in a retrieval system, or transmitted in any form or by any means electronic or mechanical or by photocopying, recording, or otherwise without prior permission of the publisher. Exclusive worldwide content publication / distribution by TotalRecall Publications, Inc.

Copyright © 2018 by: Harold Raley

ISBN: 978-1-59095-443-0
UPC: 6-43977-44432-5

Library of Congress Control Number: 2018948951

Printed in the United States of America with simultaneous printings in Australia, Canada, and United Kingdom.

FIRST EDITION
1 2 3 4 5 6 7 8 9 10

Judgments as to the suitability of the information herein is the purchaser's responsibility. TotalRecall Publications, Inc. extends no warranties, makes no representations, and assumes no responsibility as to the accuracy or suitability of such information for application to the purchaser's intended purposes or for consequences of its use except as described herein.

The scanning, uploading and distribution of this book via the Internet or via any other means without the permission of the publisher is illegal and punishable by law. Please purchase only authorized electronic editions and do not participate in or encourage electronic piracy of copyrighted materials. Your support of the author's rights is appreciated.

To Vicky

Non omnis moriar
(I shall not wholly die)
Horace

Table of Contents

Introduction: Paradox and Protagoras v
Part I: 0
The Radical Narrative 1
   1. Knocks, Noises, and Forbidden Questions 1
   2. The Abbreviated Narrative 18
   3. A Tipping Point 30
   4. Beyond Realism and Idealism 62
Part II: 78
The Structure of Mortal Life 79
   5. Saving the Circumstances 79
   6. The Missing Dimension 84
   7. Worldly Installation and Mortal Finalities 93
Part III: 142
The Immortal Narrative 143
   8. The Passing of Soledad 143
   9. Justifying Mortality 149
   10. Immortality: The Converging Evidence 156
Conclusion: 164
What is Time? Who is God? 165

Introduction: Paradox and Protagoras

We are born to live but destined to die. On this seeming paradox hang the fate of mankind and the theme of this writing. If life appears to be a miracle of creation, as we say, death seems to be a tragedy of annihilation, as we dread. In the interval we ask the primal human questions: What is man? What is our purpose? And what becomes of us? Yet these questions themselves may be clues to their answers. For would it occur to us to ask them did we not sense that life is more than mortality? Dare we then speak of immortality? Dare we not?

We have conflicting answers to these questions, but they are framed by larger uncertainties. Over the ages religious masters have taught that we are immortal beings who shuffle off this mortal coil and survive to live in another time and another place. But where is that time and place, and in what manner shall we live there? Dissenting secular thinkers tell us that the brief interval between birth and death is our only life. The human yearning for immortality contends with evidence against it, and we are perplexed. Whom and what shall we believe? Enduring doubts beg the question whether we can test the truth of our convictions or know anything for certain about our postmortem destiny.

What we do know for certain is that everyone dies. Not only are we mortal but also *moriturus*, meaning that we must die: *Mors certa, hora incerta* [certain death at an uncertain hour] according to the ancient Roman saying. We live unto death. But what is death? If we live only to perish completely then all our striving comes to naught, our immortal hopes fade into mortal darkness, and "the paths of glory lead only to the grave." "Eat, drink, and be merry," is an ancient remedy for looming death. Certainly we may eat and drink, but can we really be merry if we know that sooner rather than later death crashes our party and ends our gaiety?

This brings us to another question as old as human awareness: is death the total cessation of our life or a transition to another state of being? If our destiny be the former, then there is really little more to say, for death would mean personal annihilation and the end of our story. But if the latter proves true, then there is everything to say, for instead of personal finality, death would be a turning of the page in our continuing narrative.

So it is that questions about life, death, and purpose go in circles and we come back to where we started none the wiser for all our ponderings, except the realization that without new insights it is an idle exercise to rehash the old arguments for and against immortality. Faith alone is left to plead the immortal hope, but often it wavers and sometimes it withers.

New insights into human life made available in modern and post-modern times are the justification for this book. Intellectual honesty does not allow us to claim more than these insights and their implications can deliver. What they offer is stronger evidence of what Plato called the "exhilarating possibility of immortality."

These new insights do not replace or oppose traditional faith but support it instead. The Judeo-Christian Scriptures tell us that the prime imperative of true worship is to love God with all our heart, mind, and strength, and our fellow humans as ourselves. Like all true love, it holds nothing back but commits the entirety of life to its fulfillment. True love is total love. This writing grows out of obedience to that imperative by exploring and explaining as best this writer can some of its everlasting possibilities reached through scientific rationality and new philosophical insights into human reality.

In seeking certainties about human destiny, we necessarily expose ourselves to error. Skeptics would say ours is the supreme error of believing the fable of immortality. But skepticism is often disguised hubris, the ever-ready snare of haughty, incautious human intelligence. In any case, rightly understood, error is not necessarily failure, and failure itself need not be a dead end, but rather stages in the search for truth. The "sure step" of progress in truthful knowledge that philosopher Immanuel Kant spoke of makes no sense without possible missteps in the process, else not only would we be unable to distinguish between the sure and unsure but also would perceive no reason to do so in the first place. In any case, we cannot know one step from another unless we are bold to take them. Authentic thinking is always an exercise in courage.

The first of the primal questions posed above is probably the most fundamental of those errors. Over the ages in jest or exasperation people have asked, <u>what</u> is man?[1] Consequently there are many definitions of <u>what</u> we are: creatures of dust, brainy primates, naked apes, freaks of nature, beings "darkly wise and rudely great." In this book we center our attention on a more important question: <u>who</u> is man? Protagoras said that "Man is the measure of all things." Plato and later thinkers took his

---

[1] As the context calls for it, "man" retains, or regains, its historical Germanic sense of "one," that is, a human of either gender. Compare the German words *man* and *Mann*. The first refers to a person of either gender, the second, to a human male. Too bad English, sister language to German, did not adopt this simple way to clarify the contemporary misunderstanding of the two meanings of "man."

words to mean that truth is not absolute but relative to each person, as the Greek sophists taught in their day and neo-sophists repeat in ours. But he may have meant something altogether different, as we shall see in this essay: namely, that human life is unique and incomparably distinct from all others. But if so, the full meaning of his insight did not become apparent until our time. Human reality was not satisfactorily defined then or now, and for a good reason: definition is limitation, and human life consists of limitless, undefinable dimensions. Consequently, thinkers have alternated between timeless truth about mankind far from life and limited truth that spirals out of life's vortex. Each version surrenders what the other keeps, and neither tells us who we are.

Today it seems apparent that Protagoras said more than he knew, as we often do in moments of high inspiration. At these privileged moments it is not man who finds truth, but truth that finds man. And truth clarifies the depths, as falsehood muddies the shallows. Instead of conceding human truth to the neo-relativists or confining philosophies of the human person to contemporary sidebars—linguistic deconstructionism; existential relativism; various analytics; biological, psychological, political, and economic theories, gender topics, cosmological debates, and so on—this book centers on the reality of personhood, not for the purpose of resurrecting old relativisms but of subsuming them in a very different perspective. If man is the measure of all things, as Protagoras proclaimed, and the proper study for mankind, as Alexander Pope wrote, then how is this so and what does it mean for us? The rest of this book is my response to these questions.

Keep in mind that these questions pertain not to abstract

humanity but achieve validity in our actual life and circumstances. Many kinds of reality require abstraction in order for us to manipulate them intellectually. For instance, by means of the symbolic language of mathematics we can measure and describe the mass and velocity of astral bodies that are infinitely beyond our physical strength and engineering means to do so. In great measure advancement in science and engineering consists of the progressive substitution of symbolic manipulation for physical power. The same is true of technological enhancement. In nature man is a feeble creature; the cheetah outruns him; the eagle overflies him; the shark swims circles around him. But enhanced by his technology, man is enabled to fly higher than the eagle, outrace the cheetah, and outswim the shark. Instead of defining the human species as <u>homo sapiens</u> ["wise man"], perhaps a better scientific term would be <u>homo technicus</u>" ["technical man"].

We remind ourselves also that these symbolic substitutions are not the realities and powers they describe. If they were and the physical world at large obeyed on a universal scale these miniature manipulations, then we would be dealing with a power closer to magic than to science. Mathematics can only describe, measure, and extrapolate. Its control is symbolic. Otherwise it would be similar to a shaman who beats drums and performs rituals to frighten away demons that seem to be devouring the sun during a solar eclipse. The shaman and his people may indeed believe that he has repelled the demons when the sun emerges from the shadow. But believing it does not make it so. The physicist knows better because he understands the difference between substitutionary and physical manipulation of reality. And knowing the difference he is able to predict—though not to direct—the trajectories of astral bodies.

For this reason, the higher understanding of realities requires that we keep in mind the limitations of abstractions and the realities from which they were abstracted in the first place. Wisdom, the refinement of knowledge, consists of completing the circle by referring abstracted concepts to their original provenance reinvested with human significance.

Here I acknowledge unpayable debts owed to many philosophers, theologians, pastors, scientists, artists, writers, family, friends, and people in many occupations. We are all debtors, and like all debts, ours cannot be paid retrospectively but only prospectively, that is, paid forward as a legacy to those who will replace us.

In a particularly intense way that deserves special mention the complementary philosophical insights into human reality, specifically human life and the human person, reached in this book grow out of the groundbreaking work of two philosophers, José Ortega y Gasset (1883-1955) and Julián Marías (1914-2005). To their coordinated efforts—the intrinsic and empirical theories of human reality, respectively—I shall add further interpretations and amplifications in this writing. Unable to repay these thinkers in person, I can at least obey their joint mandate: to go on thinking, not as well as they, not as masterfully, not as creatively, but at least with the lesser gifts of acknowledgement and gratitude for their pioneering work.

Part I:

The Radical Narrative

1. Knocks, Noises, and Forbidden Questions

Philosopher José Ortega y Gasset, or simply Ortega as he came to be known, said that in order to understand anything truly human we must tell a story. Although this narrative approach resonates with my earlier comments on symbolic abstraction, it seems to contradict our modern assumptions about human reality. Usually we associate storytelling with pleasurable pastimes—and in English often with lying—not with the rigorous science, theology, and philosophy that furnish most of our conventional understanding of human life. I shall devote portions of this book to human life as a narrative or storied reality. Rightly and rigorously understood, it leads, or can lead, to what I have come to believe is a clearer way of thinking about human reality and a more enlightened understanding of our human condition and possible immortal destiny.

The first task of responsible thinking of any sort consists of justifying its reason and purpose for being. For this reason, at the beginning of this book I must ask, as the reader must wonder, is any of this necessary and justifiable? In Western culture—the general context of this writing—we already have two overarching theories of human life: theological and scientific, with the occasional convergences and contributions of several philosophies that span both categories. Is there room or reason for yet another? Consider the following points as a response to the question.

First, this book is not an argument against scientific or theological truth. Instead, I appeal to both without conscious prejudice to either. And with them I shall include the insights offered by several philosophers without whose work I could add little of substance in this writing. For untold millions of people religious teachings and traditions regarding human life are enough to live by, and for many Christian believers the Judeo-Christian Bible alone suffices. And the same is true of scientific explanations for countless people.

Second, religious belief may take many forms contained in many dogmas, and common sense tells us that not all of them can be true. Indeed, if a dogma is true, that is, demonstrably and evidentially true, then it is logical to suppose that opposing dogmas must be untrue, or at least adulterated by untruth. This is why religion, claimant to the greatest truths, may also be the guardian of the greatest falsehoods. As for science in purest form, it progresses by trial and error. What appears to be the final word today gives way tomorrow to further advances. And being a human endeavor, it is not without its own human prejudices, dogmas, and untruths.

It has become a platitude to say that no real conflict exists between religion and science. Philosophy usually has been a lesser player in the debate about origins and human life. Although philosophers have debated the meaning of truth and the problems of mankind, until recent times they have made a weak case for the special status or category of human life itself. In any case, procedurally science is the polar opposite of religion. Religion begins with revealed truth, or at least what faithful religionists believe to be true, and accommodates all realities and events in its dogmas, while defending it against internal heresies and rival theologies. On the other hand, Science begins with doubts and uncertainties, often with ignorance, and progresses toward truth by means of tentative hypotheses, and insofar as possible with verifying or disqualifying experimentation. In this book, philosophy takes the lead in the quest for understanding, but toward the end the other players, science and religion, will enter the scene to make a triple affirmation of immortality.

Because scientific truth and its premises are primarily a product of human ingenuity and an ethically neutral method, it can be shared by the bitterest of enemies and applied indiscriminately to a multitude of noble and nefarious purposes. On the other hand, religious truth with its prime concern for human fate and its claims of divine pedigree must guard not only against heresies but also ethical compromises that violate its moral doctrines. Leonardo da Vinci, for instance, was a Christian believer and as far as we know did not question the sanctity of human life inherent in the Christian faith. Yet as a scientist he applied his scientific genius to the creation of lethal instruments of war and destruction.

The intellectual terrain on which these doctrines vie is a perilous place for the timid. Faith may falter and dogmas fade when confronted with well-crafted concepts for which they are unprepared. It is a common experience for many university students, whose unexamined childhood beliefs often wilt under the pressure of sophistical ideas and sophist professors. While some students remain rooted in their first faith and beliefs, it is more likely in today's intellectual climate for them to emerge from the university in one of two extreme mindsets: (1) a dogmatic intolerance of their former beliefs, for what we cease to believe we usually scorn; or (2) what we could call "dogmatic tolerance" of the intolerable.

To reject the positions just written, as wiser, experienced persons often do in time, is to argue implicitly for a synergistic approach that marshals all available sources of truth—scientific, religious, philosophical—in clarifying human destiny or anything else. And we should add intuitive and artistic insights to the list. The more sources of authentic knowledge we have, the better our chances of discovering the truth. Judeo-Christian teaching is for many of us a revered, hard-won treasury of truth. Yet it has limits. It cannot tell us how to build an airplane, a space station, or instruct a surgeon in performing brain surgery. What it can do, and has done, is provide the light by which mankind learns to do these things.

The search for truth requires candor, which implies the boldness to say it. Surely it is no accident of history that those areas of the world where Judeo-Christian ideals prevail, or have prevailed, have also been the most creative and active in developing new sciences and technologies and in promoting human ideals of life, liberty, and the pursuit of happiness. This is why Western lapses into despotism and the toleration of intolerable ideologies are especially heinous. Of all people, Christianized or once Christianized Westerners should know better, having benefitted from spiritual, cultural, and economic advances that have transformed the world like no other. Simply by being, or having been, exposed to these Judeo-Christian influences, people develop an exalted concept of the sanctity of life, become aware of certain dimensions of reality, have insights and inspirations, and understand forms of proof and evidence natively unapparent to people in cultures lacking this experience. By a process of ethical and technological adaptation these elevated views have become either predominant in many parts of the world or acknowledged negatively by the hostility they arouse in repressive regimes, ideologies, and religions. And although these ideals often suffer distortion and abuse, at least today we ought to have the moral insight to recognize misuse, abuse, and deception for what they are. We of the West err still, but we also know error when we see or commit it and have—or have had—a collective conscience and voice to remind us when we go astray.

What is true of the Judeo-Christian tradition applies at a different but complementary level to the Classical influences in Western culture. The Greek thinkers were the first to express curiosity about the world for purely intellectual reasons. People of other ancient cultures traveled abroad to trade, conquer, and colonize. So did the Greeks, but they also had other aims; they visited foreign lands to see how other people lived and thought, and were fascinated by much of what they observed. Phoenician traders sailed out of the Mediterranean Sea and on to Britain to barter for tin. The Greeks also sent a ship past the Gates of Hercules with a philosopher aboard, but instead of a commercial duty, his purpose was to see whether it was true as rumored that the sun sizzled as it sank into the western ocean. The curious Greeks calculated the spherical shape and size of the earth with remarkable accuracy, speculated about things as remote from common need as the age and formation of the Nile Delta and the atomic structure of matter. This tradition of disinterested curiosity is a formative—and normative—element of Western civilization and an essential component of the dynamic symbiosis of religion, science, and reason. The West came to exalt the human person, and more than any other culture celebrated the genius of mankind and looked to the human mind for answers to human questions and quandaries. This was not, as it might first appear, a lack of faith in Deity. Quite the contrary; The West saw in man an epitome of the divine creative mind and spirit. Shakespeare speaks for the West in Hamlet: "What a piece of work is man! how noble in reason! how infinite in faculty! in form and moving how like an angel! in apprehension how like a god! the beauty of the world! the paragon of animals!"

The West has a dual depth that resists summary definitions. We could say metaphorically that the West began as a tale of two cities: Jerusalem and Athens, respectively representing Judeo-Christian theology and Greek philosophy and science. Remove them from history and likely we would be intellectual midgets and ethical primitives. This is why as a general pattern Westerners and non-Westerners alike must go to Western libraries, laboratories, and universities for information about the non-Christianized regions of the world. Other cultures have learned to imitate but not yet to match the special cultural blend characteristic of the Hellenized and Christianized world. For instances, other cultures are usually reluctant to underwrite salaried leisure time for researchers concerned with things that may never yield tangible results nor practical returns on the investment of resources. However, as new technologies emerge at an astonishing pace in the Western disinterested scientific curiosity and research, non-western countries require frequent technological transfusions from the West in order to keep up. They do not fully understand—and often neither do many Westerners—the real but subterranean links between imagination, spirituality, and technology.

Because we are too culturally inhibited in this self-conscious age of ours to describe many things as they really are, with considerable self-disparagement we call this phenomenon alternately the "Westernization" or more likely in recent decades the "Americanization" of the world. Ours is the first culture I know of to be embarrassed by its own greatness. But even this self-effacement is a moral remnant of Judeo-Christian enlightenment, though perhaps among its least admirable features. Dimmer in our day, it glows still.

I shall repeat from varying perspectives in this book that there is much in human life that is not human at all and that the survival of our higher human qualities is not guaranteed. I emphasize the point because these impersonal elements distort the human story, causing it to veer off into the detracting sidebars and misleading suppositions that often pass for understanding. For instance, we are inundated with information, but experience exposes much of it as misinformation. We know many things, but a good many of them are wrong and eventually we shall have to cast them off or suffer the ruination they wreak. The task is not easy; as any teacher knows by experience, false knowledge is more tenacious than simple ignorance. For this reason, it is wise to pause often in our headlong life, as the poet Antonio Machado urged, in order "to distinguish the voices from the echoes." That being the case, our first need in telling the human story—the general context of this book—is a clear distinction between human reality and the vast non-human category we call "everything else."

Fortunately, as philosopher Julián Marías reminds us, the fundamental distinction was made for us ages ago. If there is a knock on the door, we ask, "Who is it?", and expect to hear a human voice or see a person if we open it. But if something falls on the roof, our question is a startled "What was that?" In the first instance, we perceive that a knock on the door indicates an intelligent personal presence. But because we do not associate the second sound with human rationality, we switch automatically from "who?" to "what?"

This unthinking distinction between persons and things, between <u>who</u> and <u>what</u>, is as old as human experience and clear in all the languages I know anything about. It is our primary metaphysical classification, the great divide between the two general categories of reality, compared to which all other classes and levels of differentiation are secondary, despite their greater complexity, or perhaps because of it. There has always been a tendency to overlook this commonsense difference and to confuse persons who knock on doors with things that fall on roofs. And probably never more so than in our time. The modern ideological totalitarians, whose common bond is a scorn of Judeo-Christian respect for persons, describe people they consider undesirables not as persons but as mere combinations of chemicals, expendable economic units, pawns, or servants of the State. For their part, Darwinist evolutionists classify humans as peculiar primates, and having herded mankind back to nature's preserve, leave it at that. But the story of mankind begins where arguments for evolution end. Darwinism is at most a prologue, not the text.

Yet these are not the only ones who have consistently distorted human reality. For thousands of years and with the best of intentions, philosophers, prophets, and theologians have been asking, "What is man?" And by asking the wrong question, got wrong answers. Plato's definition of man as "a biped without feathers" received the ridicule it deserved when Diogenes reportedly tossed a plucked chicken in the circle of Athenian philosophers with the statement, "Plato, behold your man!"

The biblical writers fared even worse. To the vexing question they put to God, "what is man, that thou are mindful of him? and the son of man, that thou visitest him?" they received the disheartening answer that man is dust and to dust he returns at death. But <u>who</u> man is corresponds to a different question and elicits a hopeful response that fills the vast chronicles of secular history and sacred prophecy.

This simple linguistic distinction gives us our first clue to the uniqueness of human reality. Consider how differently we treat other realities that correspond to *what?* For instance, diagrams are enough to show what triangles, circles, or rectangles are. Geological science will tell us most of what we need to know about rocks and rivers, and astrophysics reveals the composition of stars and galaxies. As we progress up the scale of living creatures, however, the process becomes increasingly complex. In order to understand mammals, we need to know their genus and species, physical characteristics, range, and behaviors. Unlike humans, individual animals in the wild are nameless and generic, though we may partially personalize them, as we do with our pets, by naming them and lending them a biography. A tiger removed from its natural habitat and imprisoned in a zoo is a pathetic caricature of itself; but in the wild it is a repetition of the same great cat that stalked its prey thousands of years ago.

But, you may ask, couldn't we say the same thing about our human ancestors who lived millennia ago? When we look out on the natural world today is it not the same and do we not see it with the same human eyes with which our ancestors saw it many centuries ago? No, not altogether. We may optically see the same or similar rivers, seas, and mountains, but we understand them very differently and call them by different words with altered meanings. Today we have different scientific insights and economic purposes. A tiger roars and kills the same from age to age and thousands of years later has the same primordial instincts and appetites as its ancestors. But humans speak in many tongues and intonations corresponding to changing moral codes and advanced intellectual understandings. Though possessing instinctive maternal affection and demonstrating herd loyalty in some cases, the higher animals demonstrate only bare rudiments of oral communication and technology, and no aptitude at all for the higher human disciplines of history, literature, art, music, philosophy, science, ethics, law, mathematics, or religion. Beyond his mammalian condition—which we recognize as a real condition if we are honest with ourselves—man is also a person, a man or woman, boy or girl, with a name and a story. And primarily so; man is a biological species but also and more importantly, a biographical human person. To put it another way, man is an animal, yet one that lives a human life. Humanity contains animal biology but continues on to uniqueness and further revelation where biology stops.

This means that humans live simultaneously at two varying levels: the natural and the supra-natural. From another perspective, Christianity and some other religions acknowledge the paradoxical combination of the Old Man obedient to natural lusts and the New Man responsive to a supra-natural spiritual calling. Everything truly human is above nature as we generally understand it, yet for this very reason ever susceptible to nature's downward pull, which like another kind of gravity, would bind us anew to the natural realm. To yield to it is our original and abiding sin. Animals cannot fall because they have never risen. they simply live submerged in Nature, whereas humans live in conflictive and polarized tension between "the call of the wild," as writer Jack London described it, and the haunting possibilities of higher ideals.

By animal standards, human infancy is abnormally long but personally necessary. Unguided by instinct, which is as vestigial in mankind as legs on a serpent, we must teach and learn everything human. This means on the opposite ledger of liabilities that we may also forget or abandon the lessons. Being human is also the responsibility of remaining human and the potential irresponsibility of sloughing or degrading our human qualities.

Abandonment of our higher condition has happened before. History and prehistory tell of varying degrees of cultural lapses and reversals. According to Plato, the Egyptian priests told Solon's ancestor that the Greeks were mere children who knew of only a single age of greatness. But in their much older chronicles the Egyptians recounted many human risings and fallings in ages past. A few generations after the Golden Age of Greek philosophy, science, and learning—Pericles, Socrates, Plato, Pythagoras, Protagoras, Aristotle—incurious peasants, indifferent to ancestral greatness, plowed where their forebears once debated the seminal ideas of Western civilization. When Spanish Europeans reached the Mayan heartland in the sixteenth century, they discovered that the surviving people had long since forgotten the science, writing, and astronomy on which their classic culture once was based. They dwelt amid residual ancestral splendor but no longer possessed it. Supra-natural humanity is a tale of shifting levels, of risings and fallings, of jurisdictions formed and failed. There are no givens, no constants, and no guarantees of continuity. A single irresponsible generation is enough to start humanity backsliding to the jungle. Humanity is tenacious yet tenuous; its survival requires constant vigilance and continuing effort. With every generation humanity is put on trial. Some nineteenth-century writers of the naturalistic school described man as the "human beast." They exaggerated: man is not a beast, but he can be bestial.

But though Nature strives always to draw us back to her domain, mankind may escape its bonds. Although we may squander our humanity in spiritual and intellectual sloth and error, we can regain it by the change of heart and renewed effort we call repentance, a possibility denied to animals. Neither moral advancement nor intellectual slippage appears to be a part of their nature. Commonly we understand the transformation called repentance in a personal religious context and under certain conditions. But it is possible at any time across the whole spectrum of individual and collective human life. Of all the earthly species, only we paradoxical humans are free singly and individually to change our mind and our course. For though we have appetites and urges, we lack the instinctive nature to channel them, only the instructive technical models and ethical resources that our human culture and history offer us. As Ortega once put it, man has no nature, only a history, that is, his inherited traditions, crafts, beliefs, religions, and technologies. Without these unique human achievements, we do not, like Hollywood's Tarzan, revert to the natural state of animals as the evolutionists and naturalists used to teach, but become human monsters reckless of man and nature, as modern history shows. For though we are biologically an animal—or better said, also an animal—

we cannot live a human life as animals, just as we cannot live an animal life without natural instincts. This means that we can always fall and be less than we are, but also rise and be more than we are.

This is why scientific descriptions of man the animal falls short of describing man the human person. To know a tiger is to know what it is and likely will forever be; knowing persons is knowing who they are, have become, are still becoming, and are capable of becoming. This means that our knowledge of human life is never complete, not even in the case of those closest and dearest to us. As a novelist or an artist might say, our life is a work in progress, and the plot may turn in a multitude of directions and take on many hues and colorings. Personal human life consists of a spectrum of options and possibilities denied to animals. Man is <u>what</u> he is and he shares a part of this natural level of being with animals. But at a higher level he is more properly <u>who</u> he is, which includes the measureless potential of who he may become. His life has a unique futuristic dimension unknown in the animal kingdom. For this reason, the ancient Greeks, Aristotle, for example, wisely withheld definitive judgments about living persons. Wisely, because final acts and decisions may ennoble or annul the significance of their life. For as a story, a drama, the beginning of human life is understandable only in light of its final mortal chapter. Hence the urge to inscribe our minimal narratives in obituaries, on tombstones or burial urns, and why also the unwitnessed or unverified death or unmarked tomb of a person—an unknown soldier, for instance—leaves us with a troubling sense of human incompletion and loss. The human story, like all stories, mediocre or magnificent, has a beginning, a plot development, and a dénouement. But unlike fictional narratives circumscribed by reality, it also calls for witness and testimony to its significance and legacy. Whether the narrative matters, or can matter, to persons beyond their mortal life remains conjecturable, but it matters in this life, and it matters to us who share, witness, or love persons here and now.

As we shall see, the human relationship to time is quite different from that of animals. Pending later clarification, we can say at this point that human life not only passes in time in the animal mode but also exhibits a peculiar human immersion in time undetectable in other forms of life, even those anatomically closest to us.

For these and other reasons, the existential philosophers were wrong in their insistence on total human isolation and loneliness. We may feel ourselves isolated and lonely but it is because we sense the presence of other people at the verge of our life and because we need them in order to be ourselves. True, we may be separated from them, but "from" is both ablative and conjunctive, both separating and linking. The very absence of others indicates the empty silhouette of their presence, as the darkness of night is defined by the appositional light of day. It takes others, present by their absence, for us to feel isolated.

These human linkages are immeasurably vast and enriching. They are pathways that allow imaginary transmigration to other lives, other human narratives, and friendships with people we may never see in this world but which we need in order to relieve the common, insipid limitations of life. For all our perennial fascination with animals, they are not enough. The gulf between animals and us feeds our sense of loneliness. As humans we are alone in the world, which is why we long to know if there are other beings like us out in the Cosmos. If we are truthful about what we see animals do, we must confess an impression of their extreme limitation. This is why regardless of our love for them, somewhat similar to our love for small children, they cannot really be our equals and friends. One of the reasons they are dear to us is that like human toddlers, they are unaware of their limited life, which arouses in us a compassion, often a pity, to shield them from harm while enjoying their simple, loyal, joyful behavior.

After a short youthful period of playfulness, adult animals spend their life in restricted states of being: seeking to mate, searching for food, and avoiding becoming food themselves. In the wild, animals are often aggressive, yet seldom courageous. Instead, except for the strongest, most live fearfully alert to predators. Nor do animals spend long waking hours engaged in the creative tasks that are characteristic of humans but tend instead to spring into sudden action only to go dormant almost as quickly when things are still. Even though we surmise by their twitches and movements that some mammalian species dream—dogs for example—as far as we can tell, they do not have flights of imagination and fancy that in humans may develop into art, science, and tangible creations. Everything truly animal responds to an appetite; anything truly human begins as a dream.

Without our imaginative transmigration to other lives, times, and worlds, creative human life as we know it would be impossible and we would be temporally limited and cosmically alone. Untold damage has been done and much misinformation spread about human life by trying to interpret personal reality according to the impersonal category of things that fall mindlessly on roofs. What readily applies to impersonal things falls short when it comes to the higher human reality that knocks intelligently on doors.

Apart from some religious doctrines and specialized branches of medicine and psychology—psychiatry in particular—which incorporate patient narratives in their methodologies, our sciences, philosophies, and ideologies seem farther than ever from a comprehensive narrative of human reality. These disciplines afford us useful information about <u>what</u> we are as biological organisms, animals, and species, or as political, economic, or psychological beings, but much less about <u>who</u> we are as real persons of bone and blood, as men and women with names, dates, and biographies. In this regard, priests, poets, artists, novelists, dramatists, historians, and biographers generally—though not always—have come closest to grasping the paradoxically beautiful, complex mystery of the human person. What they do intuitively, spiritually, or artistically I am attempting to approximate in an abbreviated philosophical way in this writing.

In the life of instinct-guided animals the world repeats and ends for them unchanged. But we humans resist such futility. There is a human imperative to matter, to make a mark, to achieve something worthy of one's life. For in a vague way that often we do not fully understand, we are recipients—at least ideally—of a humanized past, heirs to what mankind has created and salvaged from oblivion over the ages, as the first recorded historian Herodotus set out to do. We respond to an urge to make our contribution, to prolong our being. And if we fail to try, we fail ourselves and our culture. Human culture is the intellectual and spiritual wealth we inherit with the obligation and options to preserve, increase, or squander.

In this sense, our life began before we did, as German historian-philosopher Wilhelm Dilthey taught. Even though we lack an instinctive nature, we have something indescribably superior: a history, the rich, effervescent alchemy of many lives that shaped ours before we were born. To them we owe not only our biological being but also our language, customs, theology, prohibitions, arts, stories, legends, knowledge, tools, technologies, and channels of being. Human maturity is the process of taking creative possession of our inheritance. On the other hand, even though animals have a chronological past, it is not historical but instinctual. So-called "natural history" is a misleading term. Essentially every animal is a repetition of the first animal. It lives instinctively through time without significantly modifying it with identifiable individual advancement. And humans who forget their history may be condemned to nearly the same fate. George Santayana declared in his celebrated maxim that those who forget their history are doomed to repeat it. But probably it is more accurate to say that those who squander their history will not have a chance to repeat it. In any case, Cicero probably told a greater truth when he observed that people without a knowledge of history remain immature children. For children are those who spend their childhood learning and rehearsing the preliminaries. As historical beings, we live in the depth and height of time, and as we claim it, we also must assume responsibility for it. Not only do we stand figuratively on the shoulders of the generations that preceded us, but in us their ambitions find fulfillment or lie fallow. Each life, each person, adds to, or erases a page and a portion of the universal narrative. The fulfillment of each human life and each collectivity is needed to compose the general human narrative, and each omission or failure is a human loss that sends a disturbing tremor through the Cosmos. Being human is being responsible, and responsibility is inescapably moral, a series of repeating decisions about what is preferable or unworthy. This means, considered negatively, that immorality is always by commission or omission a human possibility that trails us like our shadow in the sunlight.

In our simple, unthinking way, we take the first step in this form of understanding every time somebody knocks on the door or something falls on the roof. There are many other stages and chapters in the human story. In this book we shall consider some and suggest others. But in order to tell the story we must reclaim the right to ask the fundamental questions that modernity forbade.

We begin by acknowledging what may be the paramount geopolitical problem of this age. In contrast to simple calendric progression, human collectivities, like human persons, have many simultaneous "ages." Some are cultural infants; others are just now entering into exuberant youth; still others have reached the settled middle stage, and lastly trail those that have begun the shrinkage of old age. It is utopian to ask the young to act old, or the old to pretend to be young. World unity may be a worthy ideal—though that remains to be seen and proved. But probably it will bring problems instead of plenitudes until cultures are free to act their age.

2. The Abbreviated Narrative

As the Modern Age peaked in full maturity in Western culture in the last years of the nineteenth century and beginning of the twentieth, the human story we are outlining was abbreviated. Intellectual leaders, primarily philosophers and scientists, first agreed, then decreed, that questions about ultimate human destiny with their heavy load of mystery and mysticism were no longer proper themes for enlightened humanity. Like a disruptive child, religious dogma was banished to a corner along with other discredited beliefs. Or, alternately, repackaged to make it appear fit for modern company.

Darwinism seemed to have settled the matter of human reality: man is one of the primates, comparatively advanced yet taxonomically still an ape. With the religious narrative seemingly discredited or reduced to an anemic ethics, metaphysical questions of human reality and destiny needed no longer to be asked, which soon was taken to mean that they should be silenced and forbidden as idle matters unworthy of enlightened minds. The matter seemed settled; Western mankind now had the only answers that mattered. The classic questions about human destiny became the forbidden questions.

It was the culmination of a process that began long before Darwin. Three hundred years earlier, René Descartes, though himself a Christian believer, raised doubt to the level of virtue and philosophic method, and as the modern age culminated, whole categories of things spiritual and intangible were removed from the intellectual panorama, or, as with Voltaire, became the butt of jokes and sarcasm. Mankind, which once stood only a little lower than angels in the theological hierarchy, rose barely higher than apes in the new Darwinian paradigm. Desmond Morris would call man the "hairless ape," and today animal rights advocates argue that the higher primates deserve civil rights similar to those accorded humans. Or to look at it from another perspective, humans had no moral right to privilege and special consideration. If anything, they deserved to be condemned as a predatory interlopers raging destructively in Nature's once paradisiacal realm. There grows in our day a nostalgic wish for a human-free paradise.

It is worth noting that often it is not the originators of new theories who take them to extremes of refinement or error but their less gifted disciples. Darwin, for example, wrote that he saw no reason why his ideas should cause anyone to question their Christian faith. On the other hand, his intellectual descendants saw no reason why people should continue to believe it.

Imperialistic exaggeration was the characteristic mindset of late Modernity. Unconscious hubris was taken to be the natural order of the age. It was the metastatic expansionism that often precedes decline. Each discipline sought to speak for all humanity and to extend its dominion over the earth. Imperialistic geopolitics had counterparts in art, philosophy, science, literature, and music. The vast musical worldview of Richard Wagner was akin in spirit to the nation-building will of Cecil Rhodes and the American imperialists. Newton and Darwin made science the apex of human inquiry, and notable inventors and powerful industrialists—Edison, Ford, Tesla, Morse, Bell— would strive to bring it to technological fruition. Meanwhile, Flaubert, Hugo, Dickens, Goethe, and their peers strode across the literary terrain like princely lords. Kant, Comte, and Hegel created vast philosophical empires. In the hands of Marx and Trotsky philosophy metastasized into mass ideology and sought to reshape the world in its image. And before Darwinism tamped Christian zeal, missionaries carried Western-style conversion, culture, and clothing to the religiously innocent of the remotest lands.

But even as missionaries were busily converting the pagan world, the Western certitudes were already showing fault lines. Generations of atheistic thinkers in science and philosophy—Bentham, Comte, Spencer, Schopenhauer, Pavlov, Croce, Haldane, Russell, Sartre, Skinner, Higgs, Dawkins, Hawking, and many others—created a new "atheistic orthodoxy" in which God was viewed not as the Creator but as a relic superstition of a bygone age. Horizontality was replacing verticality in everything from politics to poetry. Equality was the political ideal, especially among the intellectually advanced and powerful. But they hedged by thinking of themselves as first among equals. Supreme beings, like supreme monarchs, were no longer welcome, and vigilant intellectual guardians stood ready to block the return of the king. Politically, liberal democracy was leveling the world. Long political tenure was inherently dangerous to increasingly mass-dominated societies. The success of mass government depended inversely on the short tenure and early failure of politicians.

Yet as the ideal of equality of condition grew greater, so surged the competing ambition for absolute individual power. Equality was the official doctrine for the masses, but superiority was the unspoken personal ambition for the elites. After all, democracy was an elitist creation in ancient Greece as it was in modern America and Europe. The advent of democracy, which was intended to elevate the masses to the detriment of the privileged nobility, did both, but with the unforeseen consequence of creating new elites. For instance, Napoleon rose to destructive tyranny while espousing the Enlightenment ideals of equality, opportunity, and human betterment. It is debatable whether France ever recovered completely from the murder of its best and brightest in the Revolution and the slaughter of Napoleon's protracted wars. A century later, the Bolsheviks proclaimed the rights of workers, killed their rivals, and concentrated all power in an elitist dictatorship that murdered millions.

In passing, it is interesting to note in this context that in Western culture the modern centuries appear to possess gender. Generally speaking and always with exceptions, the eighteenth century was noticeably feminine and aristocratic in taste—everything truly feminine—though not every female—possesses an aura of aristocratic elegance—whereas the nineteenth-century was heavily masculine, ponderous, and pragmatic in its worldview. The eighteenth century seduced the world into civilization; the nineteenth forged it into empire. It was a competition between grace and might, and both succeeded to a remarkable degree. Today the movement toward globalization tends to gloss over the deep historical cleavage between centuries much more surely than calendar dates. More needs to be said on the matter, but we leave the task for another day.

It followed logically in this deconstruction of the older paradigms that as the image of a fatherly, forgiving God diminished in the modern centuries, mankind no longer had a guarantor of life in the Hereafter. Theology has a closer kinship with politics than we see. The foundational hope and progressive optimism of modern Western mankind entered into a long contentious decline. Questions concerning Deity and immortality became bothersome nuisances to the majority of modern intellectuals, who dismissed them outright or shunted them off to traditional theology which they regarded as the trash bin of outworn ideals.

Belief in mankind's immortal destiny slowly faded in the modern centuries. The medieval peasant might be as poor as dust, and think of himself as such, yet he could be proud of his soul, for he had the firm assurance that if he was dust in this world, in the next he could stand with popes and kings. As the medieval "Dance of Death" revealed, if mortality eventually leveled all people, great and small, God would raise them to immortal happiness and dignity in the Hereafter.

Although philosophers like Kierkegaard and Unamuno protested with strident pathos the existential death sentence of the individual person decreed by modern thinkers, in the view of social, scientific, and existential thinkers from Comte, Marx, and du Noüy to Russell, Haldane, Dawkins, and Hawking, personal survival beyond death was an absurd notion, though the same cannot be said of prolonging earthly life indefinitely. Mankind might survive collectively like an impersonal, collective beehive or as cosmic migrants—though this possibility was also problematic—but personal survival beyond common mortality was considered an affront to reason. To these modern thinkers, personal immortality made no sense in a spiritless Cosmos, the impersonal successor to the Christian cosmic paradigm. The spiritual wellspring of Western culture was running dry.

But people are persons—men and women—before they are artists, doctors, carpenters, soldiers, teachers, merchants, bankers, atheists, farmers, mechanics, philosophers, priests, scientists, beggars, or anything else, and even though they may bow to the modern dogmas and ignore the forbidden questions of human fate, these continue to act nonetheless at unspoken, subversive levels, calling into question human life. In the Modern Age never did Western mankind have more technical advantages at its disposal; never did man himself matter less. The ever-expanding dimensions of the Cosmos corresponded inversely to the ever-shrinking significance of humankind. We must wonder whether faithful medieval serfs would pity their rich but faithless modern descendants.

For want of a better name, we have tended in recent decades to call ourselves "post-Moderns." But this implies, at least linguistically, that we are anachronisms defined by who we once were but are no more. To look at it from another perspective, the term implies that now begrimed by flaws and burdened by history, as a civilization we have lived our best days. Even though our technological achievements proliferate by inertia, like a train that thunders ahead with a dead engineer at the throttle, the formative human triumphs of our civilization recede into the past as we hurtle along, driverless and heedless of destination.

Today an existential guilt has settled over the West. We regret that we have subdued and abused nature, once our most formidable foe. Once we believed that we were God's supreme creation. Now contrite, we think of ourselves as numerically excessive, abnormal animals that are environmentally destructive and existentially unjustified. We do penance not in empty churches but in abortion clinics. At one time the so-called "white man's burden" was understood as the duty to enlighten backward peoples. Now we are ashamed of our ancestral temerity to think any people backward. Today the burden of the Western white race is being white.

We are left with multiplying means but diminishing meanings. What the Modern Age once considered its highest virtues we now see as its greatest errors. And we can be certain of nothing except that to be astute is to look askance at everything we once stood for. Cynicism is our substitute for wisdom, and no one reminds us that it is the most corrosive of all errors. The only absolute truth of our time is that truth is absolutely relative, an indirect way of saying that absolute truths are absolute falsehoods, and particularly those to which we once pledged our greatest allegiance. Consequently, we are less passionate about discovering new truths than demolishing old ones. We celebrate the destruction of older absolutes as liberation and with equal zeal place the yokes of new enslaving falsehoods about our neck in the name of freedom.

But a new day breaks faintly on the horizon and we begin to discern its agenda of promises and perils. The time has come to renew the narrative and continue the human story. As its light waxes and old certitudes wane, we see that Truth is absolute after all. It is we who are its poorer relatives. Two and two still make four, not a sum of our choosing. The Modern thinkers believed the fundamental questions had been laid to rest. But if so, the corpses are stirring with new life.

Not that uncertainty and error themselves were the intellectual disgrace as both medieval and modern thinkers believed. I repeat what I wrote earlier: sure steps often involve many missteps. As far as we know, the early Greek thinkers first asked the fundamental questions that were to shape the West. And promptly came up with what to us are absurd answers. To the metaphysical question of reality, they taught variously that combinations of fire, water, earth, and air were the basic components of all things. From our perspective these were silly, simplistic hypotheses. But if we stop there, we miss the imperishable importance of their efforts. It was not that they had the right answers, but that they had begun to ask the right questions. Instead of relying on omens and oracles as their ancestors had done for uncounted ages, for the first time, men turned their intellect to the task of rationally explaining the world. And authentic philosophy and science have proceeded ever since by asking the questions, not necessarily discovering the ultimate answers. For if they had hit quickly upon the correct answers, it would have been unnecessary to repeat the prime questions, and philosophy and its descendant sciences would have died aborning. Paradoxically, both science and philosophy still exist today thanks to lingering doubt and ignorance. How so? Because we can never be certain that even our most advanced answers are ultimately the best and truest. Beyond every answer other questions arise. Beyond every truth greater truths cast their approaching shadows. The quest and the questions go on, perhaps forever. The world is always more than we know, and error keeps us moving toward its greater revelation. How miserly, how selfish, how unintelligent, therefore, to set limits and boundaries and declare like the Fool of Psalms that there is no God or truth beyond that which we have seen with our eyes, touched with our hands, or analyzed in our laboratories. Genuine metaphysics—the master science of reality—followed long enough always becomes a lesson in humility, gratitude, and enlightenment.

To deny God, as it became stylish to do in modern times, is to be intellectually responsible for proving the absence, just as to assert the existence of divinity is to assume the duty of giving similar reasons for the assertion. Intellectual justification is always a moral constant. On the other hand, intelligence ungrounded in morality often proves to be mankind's most dangerous attribute.

By common consensus modernity has run its course, and unlike what poet T.S. Eliot proclaimed, it ends with both extravagant bangs and despairing whimpers. It accomplished much and still clings to its old hegemony. But it no longer arouses our enthusiasm; its run is over, yet it lingers like guests who overstay their welcome. We live in a time no longer ours, yet feel obligated to apologize for its excesses as a first phase and to atone for them in a second. Consequently, by degrees we have come to revile our ancestors for their vices, not revere them for their virtues. The heroes of yesterday are become the villains of today. And as we cease to revere our forebears, we cease to respect ourselves.

A new age looms before us. We cannot yet call its name, for unlike infants, historical eras receive their true names in retrospect. The old certainties of modernity about the world have turned problematic and perilous, obliging us to ask anew the forbidden questions: Who am I? Who are we? Why are we here? Who or what put us here? What can we know? Can we know truth? What must we do? What will become of me and those I love? What is the meaning, if any, of what I see before me?

In their time the Moderns responded by declaring such questions moot and discouraging inquiry. But the moderns are gone and with them their prohibitions. The dead may bury their dead, but they have no right to bury us with them. Nor can they enforce their posthumous will to shape our enthusiasms, assign us our loyalties, and set our limits. A day will dawn—perhaps sooner than any can foresee—when we realize to our disgust and dismay just how bound we have allowed ourselves to become to enslaving falsehoods.

For many decades our modern forefathers could ignore the

forbidden questions. The momentum of the Christian ages long sustained Modern people drawing from deep moral and spiritual reserves. But as they ceased to sow spiritually, so they ceased to reap culturally. Eventually the reserves were depleted, and the Moderns vanished, leaving the world, as the poet Gray put it, "to darkness and to us."

Unlike the moderns, we are not without hope or means. We have new perspectives, new intuitions, and new intellectual instruments. And most of all, we have the resurrected problems and questions. Freed from the modern taboos, the way is cleared for us to set wit and heart once more to wrestling with the forbidden questions. In this spirit the wiser course is to turn away from those who continue to repeat the negative dogmas that defined the latter stages of modernity. This is particularly true of atheistic minds. It is not primarily a religious question of belief or unbelief. People will believe or doubt as their spirit inclines them. But no one has the moral or intellectual right to proclaim as unquestionable philosophical or scientific certainties what are mere private, or in many cases, inherited conjectures. More importantly, the prime intellectual imperative of genuine thinkers is to keep their mind open to the fundamental questions about human destiny and do so without deciding in advance what the acceptable answers can be, or whether reasonable answers are possible at all. History favors the procedure: far more good for humanity has come from open minds than from those dogmatically closed in any sense. The master questions remain, and perhaps forever shall in this life, to allow us to make collateral discoveries, including new ways of asking them and new perspectives from which to ask them. Willingness to keep an open mind to the forbidden questions is not truth itself, but it allows us to search for truth more efficiently and recognize it more readily when we find it. Categorical minds—brilliant or mediocre—are limited to their categories.

Our prospects are exhilarating. Ours is a privileged moment, as all moments are, and we are unsuited to live in any other. Living is dangerous, and doom always lurks frighteningly near or reasonably far. But the imperative to live life, brief or long, is our irrepressible response. A residue of happiness illuminates life's core, lighting our way even in darkest night to fulfill our personal mission and collective destiny.

It is not in their triumphant revolutionary proclamations and brash youthful assertions that we should judge cultures and republics, but in the just and stable sturdiness of their middle age and the mature humaneness of their final stages. For human cultures and their foundational ideals are also mortal. Human contrivances eventually fail and must yield their hegemony to new ideals.

Unless we bear this hard rule in mind, the funereal farewells and doomsday predictions that sprout from the moldering ruins of modernity may faze us. Enlightenment historian Edward Gibbon considered Rome to be mankind's greatest collective creation and blamed Christianity for its downfall. But on the ruins of Classical civilization Christians wrought greater works than Rome. And so it has ever been; such demises have proved to be preludes to future resurrections. The human journey, the story and inherent drama of human life goes on, despite frequent Gibbonesque predictions of apocalyptic finalities. The odds that demolish one age become the birth pangs of the next. Birth and death alike are often painful, but for the grateful of heart the lively interval between more than compensates for the distress, and we must learn again that despair is akin to blasphemy. How often men have foretold the end of all things good and lovely and true. Yet the night passes, the sun still rises, the golden years return, and the earth recovers its splendor. It takes a winter to have a spring and a death to have a resurrection.

3. A Tipping Point

Here we begin to compose the human melody in a different key. As we set out to explore what the title means, keep in mind a preliminary observation that has a bearing on later concepts. Like all human reality, authentic thought is a matter of levels, not editorial deference to dates, schools, or academic manuals, though these have their importance. The quality of human creations—art, mathematics, music, philosophy, science, law, literature, governance, statecraft—is not primarily a function of its date of emergence into public awareness. In the long run, it consists of their level and content. We all know that in many cases recent entry foretells a hasty disappearance. A good many novelties that respond to the mass tastes in our time— music, movies, toys, fashions—commonly have only seasonal appeal. In some cases, their *éclat* barely survives a daily headline or soundbite and in a week is relatively older than the Great Pyramid of Giza, which is still the latest word in pyramids. Time commonly grinds slowly with great realities, but with less substantial things it is an impatient disqualifier that quickly sweeps them away, as a wind gust carries away rootless debris. Consumerism, the modern capitalistic phenomenon of rapid production and quick obsolescence of products, also applies to people and relationships—marriage, friendship, entertainment, ideas, and almost anything else that defines the configuration of the mass taste in our day. There is a compelling urge to keep up with styles, models, and modes, but it is a losing race. Despite all our efforts to stay up with things today, our latest fad will be fodder for tomorrow's farce.

Superior levels are an entirely different matter. The way of thinking that I shall present in this writing is, so I believe, beyond the conventional consumerist time lines of this era. We might be tempted to describe it as timeless but for the fact that it is archly timely, more so than any modern philosophical advance that I know of. This means that it resists rapid obsolescence but also quick popularity. But let us reserve these arguments for the proper moment. We have time, which means that we can exercise the virtue of patience. These assertions may invite mockery. But as the poet Horace said ages ago, "Why do you laugh at my story? With the proper adjustments, the tale is about you."

This brings up another matter of wider consequences. Superior insights in any discipline immediately make lesser concepts dated, even the latest ones. The reasons for this are not always clear. The collective consciousness, like the ocean level, is not deceived. It readily detects whether an idea is below the real level of the times and begins its implacable tidal readjustment. It is not that people necessarily have better knowledge, only that they sense the inadequacy of what is consensual. Often the latest things are already relics, and in ways not easily explainable. This is why, to give it a specific intellectual context, it can be argued that the reason contemporary American and European philosophy has such a negligible impact on society and why the little influence it enjoys is nearly always negative and humanly belittling, is that it is below the figurative oceanic level of our time. In the most accurate sense it is reactionary regardless of its ideological or political tilt. Why so? Because it would hold us, or take us back, to who and where we have already been. And who we have been we cannot be again, at least not in the same way. As Heraclitus said ages ago, we cannot step twice in the same river, even though it bears the same name.

In this book we shall examine a radically new perspective of human life that raises understanding to a new level. As I said before, it begins with the thought of philosopher José Ortega y Gasset (1883-1955). Ortega developed his system around a collective certainty: modernity was ending, the old glories had passed away, and new ways of thinking were gestating. For Ortega the need and reality of transformation was to be his calling.

Geopolitically, it was a particularly dark period for his native Spain. Defeated in the Spanish American War of 1898, it lost its remaining overseas possessions, principally Cuba, Puerto Rico, and the Philippine Islands. Its once vast, multi-continental empire was gone. Except for small enclaves in Africa after nearly five centuries Spain was once again reduced to its European homeland and seemingly destined to remain, perhaps forever, a cultural backwater. It was an era of soul-searching and spiritual handwringing. As if the fiasco of 1898 were not setback enough, it was followed by decades of political misdirection that culminated in the Spanish Civil War (1936-39) and the Franco dictatorship, which with lessening strictness lasted until 1975.

Yet it was also an era of remarkable literary and intellectual production. It is a mistake to think that the one depends on the other. Driven back on itself, Spain reacted with an explosion of literary and philosophical genius that rivaled its two-century long Golden Age of geographical and artistic triumph (1474-1681).

Ortega was in the thick of it. He labored mightily to invigorate Spanish culture with his own thought and by inviting foreign luminaries in philosophy and science to Spain, for instance, Albert Einstein. In 1924 he added another dimension to his family's publishing empire with *Revista de Occidente*, which began as a journal and later expanded into book publishing. His school of skilled translators made books of the highest caliber available to Spanish readers. His first major work, *Meditations on Quixote* (1914) established him as Spain's leading philosopher. In it he set the premises of his philosophy which we shall summarize later in this writing.

Critics often reproach Ortega for a lack of philosophic system, while he maintained that his system was already in place as early as 1914 in his *Meditations on Quixote*. In a sense both views are valid, depending on what is meant by "system." His critics understood system to be a formal and consistent textual elaboration and organization of doctrines, whereas Ortega took the term to mean conformity to the structure of reality itself, particularly human reality. *Meditations on Quixote* is at once an aesthetically moving example of systematic descriptive phenomenology and the elevation of the method to its transcendent human significance. But the eleven lessons titled *¿Qué es filosofía?* (1929) [What is Philosophy?] fleshed out the earlier outline.

But what is phenomenology? Based on the Greek word for appearance (*phainomenon*), phenomenology has many subsequent variations, but initially it is a philosophic method of dealing with the appearance of things, objects, or circumstances in one's immediate, first-person perception. Though weighted with the prestige and murkiness of Classical Greek terminology in modern languages, descriptive phenomenology in its first phase is the straightforward, commonsense account of our personal lived experiences without abstract generalizations or prior interpretations.

German philosopher Edmund Husserl (1859-1938), who is generally acknowledged as the founder of the phenomenological school, was clear about the descriptive phase of phenomenology. But he encountered difficulties, as we shall see, when he ventured into the analysis of phenomena. Martin Heidegger (1889-1976), a one-time disciple of Husserl, taught that the revelation of phenomena was *Alétheia,* the unveiling of reality, which to the classical Greeks was truth itself. French writer Jean-Paul Sartre (1905-1980), who applied existential principles to phenomenological perceptions in his novels such as *La Nausée,* was dismayed—"nauseated"—by the fact that mankind is condemned to the cosmic abandonment called freedom.

Ortega studied philosophy in Germany (1906-07 and 1911). During his second residency he became a disciple of Husserl. But he veered away from Husserl when the latter announced his return to Cartesian thought. Ortega's use of descriptive phenomenology and the way he turned it to more hopeful conclusions in *Meditations on Quixote* opened the way to further growth and expansion of his core doctrine. In Lesson VII of **What is Philosophy?** he offered the disclaimer that he chose to remain silent about certain ideas that had been maturing in his thinking for many years, in some cases since early youth. In Lesson X, he explains that haste is not the way of the philosopher: "I am in no hurry for others to tell me I am right. Being right is not a train that departs on a fixed schedule. Only the ill and the ambitious are in a hurry." As it turned out, Ortega's words were perhaps more prophetic than he knew. Events prevented him from editing the lessons, in which he explained his system much more comprehensively than the shorter summary in *Meditations on Quixote*. Nor were they translated into English until 1958, three years after his death when his image was fading from public awareness not only in the English-speaking countries but also in Europe and even in Spain itself.

Following a series of preliminary observations in Lessons I and II on the fallacy of relativistic truth and the essential historicity of human life, in the third lesson Ortega launches his inquiry into the nature of philosophy with the framing statement that it must have as its objective nothing less than knowledge of the Universe. The scientific disciplines such as chemistry, mathematics, and particularly physics, the most prestigious science of Ortega's day—and ours—confine themselves to a circumscribed physical or theoretical field of inquiry, and while they acknowledge the valid principles and discoveries of other sciences, procedurally they utilize them only insofar as they lend support to their special objectives. Thus, a biologist may turn to mathematics to make statistical analyses, but it would be unusual for a physicist to make use of biological data, much less philosophic principles, in order to do physics.

There are, therefore, obvious differences between the objective of philosophy and the circumscribed fields and data characteristic of the individual sciences such as mathematics, chemistry, biology, or physics. Unlike the scientific territory included in these fields, which are defined by their convenient boundaries, by its very nature the philosophic enterprise encompasses everything, at least in principle, and cannot be similarly compartmentalized without surrendering its condition of philosophic universality. In theory, philosophy omits nothing real from its purview. It is precisely the cosmic entirety that it must embrace and take responsibility for intellectually. Or to put it in simpler terms, philosophy is the science of the whole. For this reason, Ortega calls the philosophical quest for clarity and veracity "theoretical heroism." The heroic and dramatic nature of philosophy appears frequently in Ortega's writings, as do its ludic and zestful characteristics. For this reason, whenever possible he wrote only when he was in top physical form and not afflicted by his frequent bouts of illness. A notable exception to this pattern is his *Meditación del marco* [Meditation on a Picture Frame], a literary marvel he produced while convalescing from an illness in a bare hospital room.

Ortega tells us that the broad latitude of the philosophic purview can never be justification for claims of superiority over the scientific researcher. On the contrary, by a formula of proportional dimensions, the greater the task, the greater the probability of error and thus the stronger the need to guard against arrogance and to cultivate a willingness for self-correction. But this attitude must not be mistaken for intellectual timidity. Philosophy requires the peculiar and seemingly contradictory combination of daring, alertness, knowledge, skill, and prudent self-control. No wonder Ortega could write so insightfully about the kinship between the alertness of the hunter and the vigilance of the philosopher in his acclaimed preface to *Veinte años de caza mayor* [Twenty Years of Big Game Hunting (1942)] or grasp analogies between the thinker standing his ground against the onrush of problems and a bullfighter facing the bull's ferocious charge. (His namesake, celebrated bullfighter Domingo Ortega, said that listening to Ortega's lectures made him a better bullfighter. His comment reminds us that both crudeness and elegance transcend their original spheres, spilling over to roughen or refine other sectors of life.)

It should be noted, however, that like other philosophers of his day—Bertrand Russell and Alfred North Whitehead in England, for example—Ortega felt the pressure and prestige of the sciences and sought to clarify the ways in which they differed from philosophy. For their part, Russell and Whitehead blurred the lines and thought it desirable to erase the classic divisions by deferring to the mathematically based sciences. On the other hand, for Ortega, the necessary dichotomy of unequal inquiries—the partial versus the whole, the scientific versus the philosophic—means that philosophy cannot properly be configured to fit the mold of scientific knowledge, even though it acknowledges their common intellectual ancestry and accepts the validity of scientific principles and discoveries. Beset by a flagging spirit, modern philosophy, particularly Anglo-American pragmatism and linguistic deconstructionist thought, has come to emulate scientific reasoning and documentation and appears eager to pass itself off as a science. Exactly what sort of science is a matter better omitted in this limited context.

Despite his own youthful socialist leanings, Ortega never allowed the political to intrude on the philosophical. His political views and activities were a function of his patriotism, only remotely of his philosophy. He always stoutly proclaimed that philosophy could not be simply another science or discipline, much less a political adjunct, not because it is less than or equal to these disciplines but because it was and had to be much more.

The philosophic endeavor differs from scientific inquiry in an even more fundamental way. If philosophy should discover, for example, that the universe is ultimately chaotic or was created by a capricious, irrational being, as the pessimistic Schopenhauer taught, then it would prove to be rationally hermetic and impenetrable and thus entirely beyond the scope of science. Nevertheless, such a discovery would constitute valid philosophy even though it would be radically different in nature from rational scientific knowledge. From its beginning philosophy cannot discard this very possibility; the universe may indeed be an unsolvable problem resistant to human rationality. But even if this were the case and Schopenhauer and similarly minded thinkers should be right, philosophy would still have fulfilled its task by demonstrating in a rational way the capricious and chaotic irrationality of the Universe.

Ortega points out that traditional Anglo-American pragmatism and similar continental doctrines avoid the possible risks of confronting such universal problems simply by declining to deal with them, while others—among them certain strains of existentialism, deconstructionism, relativism, feminist theory, and linguistic doctrines that bubble in the caldron of modern intellectual thought—go a step further by declaring *a priori* that we cannot hope to reach absolute truth or knowledge and that it is best to limit our quest before we start to a predetermined mindset that does not compromise with any subsequent option. Ortega comments disapprovingly that for these pragmatic thinkers the only valid problems are those with foreseeable, foregone conclusions. He warns that such an attitude, which may arise either from excessive caution or prior slanted persuasion, cannot be the proper cast of mind for the authentic philosopher who must have the heroic courage to take on the whole spectrum of reality without preconceived limits.

Paradoxically but amply demonstrated, the denial of certainty in the "forbidden problems" we saw earlier then becomes an odd species of reverse, or negative, dogmatic certainty that further discourages philosophic inquiry. The lack of absolute proof is taken without further ado as absolute proof of the absence of proof. For the pragmatist thinker, whose intellectual perspective derives, according to Ortega, from the practical bourgeois mindset of earlier centuries, problems are by definition those that can be solved, or at least resolved, by approaches similar to those that apply to material things. Those that would require us to transcend this limited paradigm—theological thought for instance—are thus dismissed in advance because they are declared to be formally unsolvable by means of pragmatic, conventional reasoning. Ortega argues that this restriction is contrary to the general principle of philosophic universality and effectively reduce philosophy to a field of inquiry with metes and boundaries similar to those of the scientific disciplines but without their positive attitude and results.

Although philosophy in the Ortegan paradigm claims a universal panorama, it must begin much more modestly, even self-consciously, not with the Cosmos, metaphysics, or even the investigative fields and problem-sets of the sciences but with something so obvious as to escape our notice: *the peculiar nature of philosophy itself* and its reason for being or, as the other side of the coin, the internal contradictions that threaten to annul its validity. (In a moment of pique Ludwig Wittgenstein [1889-1951, the father, or grandfather, of linguistic philosophy] reportedly commented that intellectually the most honest thing philosophers of language could do would be to remain silent.)

For Ortega the philosophic imperative means that the first task of the philosopher consists of justifying the philosophical endeavor itself. This is another way of stating that philosophy, which puts nothing off limits in its universal scrutiny—except limitation itself—requires justification as a preliminary step before it takes on the Cosmos. Before it can clarify things beyond it, philosophy must be clear about the methods inherent within it. Not that such justification is ever complete once and for all time. On the contrary, it consists of a constant process of calling into question its own theoretical assumptions. To commit oneself to thought is to commit oneself to go on thinking. Contrary to the old image of the absent-minded thinker, Philosophers must always be aware of where they are, what they are doing, and why they are doing it. Their feet must be on the ground and their vision focused on the reality at hand, not lost in the clouds. If nothing is alien to philosophy, then philosophers must be prepared to consider all realities. The foremost characteristic of this prime imperative is unrelenting alertness—similar to that of a hunter as we saw earlier—and a constant willingness to modify one's concepts or even to accept new ones. An open Cosmos finds its hospitable counterpart in an open mind.

Yet fidelity to false orthodoxies is surely among mankind's oldest intellectual and theological shortcomings. Ideally, therefore, the good that philosophy discovers must always be prepared to give way to the better; dogmatic orthodoxy must yield—ideally at least—to higher truths. Here it is important to emphasize a major Ortegan imperative. He begins this series of lessons, as he begins several of his mature writings, with the conviction that both the doctrines of realism and idealism, the alternating modes of philosophy since Classical Greece, are now outdated and must be surpassed. And he believed he was the person to do it. It was a bold ambition that Ortega never relinquished and which, at least to his own satisfaction, he achieved by absorbing them, as we shall see later, in a transcendent doctrine.

But if philosophy is by its nature an exercise in intellectual heroism, alertness, and disciplined boldness, as Ortega would have us believe, throughout the modern age classic European philosophy was characterized by a certain reluctance to venture forth into the world. Philosophers, chief among them Descartes (1596-1650), sought what Immanuel Kant would call later *der sichere Gang*, the sure step, the solid foundation capable of supporting the edifice of an unassailable philosophy. From Descartes to Husserl, including Kant and Leibniz, European philosophy was dominated by varieties of restrictive, mind-locked subjective idealism. Even though it produced splendid psychological insights in Brentano and Bergson, the introverted defensive mentality of Cartesians permeated philosophy throughout the modern era.

Descartes reasoned that the world apparent to our senses could be a Great Deceiver's deceptive trickery, and that we may be dupes of the deception. It marked the apogee of the modern fear of error—a secular echo of the medieval horror of sin—which, let us note, often outweighed the attractiveness of truth. Withdrawing into the fortress of his mind, Descartes reasoned that only one's thinking, the *cogito* [I think], is safe from deception. Though lacking spatial extension and material being that human senses attribute to physical things, thinking is more dependable than realities that possess these tangible, measurable characteristics. Moreover, even if my physical being is real, I am fragile, a mere breath of mortal life, a thing, a *roseau pensant*, a thinking reed, according to Blaise Pascal. Yet there is a certainty in the premise: *Cogito, ergo sum* [I think, therefore I am]. My thinking is self-evidently undeniable and, therefore, so is my being. The immediacy of my thought, untampered in its inwardness, at a remove from seductive deceptions possibly emanating from a malignant mind beyond me, is the only certainty on which I may rely. And by means of this Cartesian *Cogito* I may with due prudence reason my way to whatever realities may transcend me and constitute what I first and tentatively perceive by my senses to be the world. The reasonable certainty of the primal Cartesian proposition allows us to entertain subsequent declarations with cautious confidence. With such caution Descartes and his followers would go on to construct what they saw as the only trustworthy philosophy and from this unarguable idealism they would cautiously emerge to retake the extra-subjective world once lost to uncertainty, doubt, and possible deception.

Doubt had always been a reason for philosophers to detect and eliminate it. Nevertheless, the history, indeed the progress, of philosophy is also a record of repeated error. But as we saw earlier, this condition is not as grim as it first sounds, nor as repugnant as the moderns made it out to be. Human perception is historically relative, that is, relative to history. Ortega has just argued in the *Lessons* that truth does not change. What changes is our historical relationship to reality and thus also to truth. This means that the human intellect is natively susceptible to error because our perspective is limited and mutable. Cartesian genius consisted of the fact that instead of shunning or denying doubt as the fruit of error, instead of seeing it as a dreaded canker that traditionally demolished the certainty of philosophic propositions, Descartes confronted it, embraced it, and converted it into the dialectic of systematic doubt and backhanded certainty. But the immediate price he and followers paid for doing so was a provisional suspension of the sense-derived certainty of the external world of things. Later, with the appearance of Husserlian phenomenology, it seemed that modern philosophy was in danger to being reduced to mere thinking about thought itself, as Husserl put it, *Cogito cogitatum* [I think about thinking].

Ortega and several young German classmates were deeply impacted by phenomenology. Infatuated might be a better description. In fact, some scholars have argued that Ortega remained a phenomenologist for the rest of his life, but the argument falls from the weight of evidence against it, even though it is true that phenomenology was the springboard from which Ortega launched himself into his own philosophy, and phenomenological description with modifications was incorporated into his doctrine.

Though a summary and not yet a comprehensive description of his system, *Meditations on Quixote* was the first mature level of his philosophy. Mature, yet it was to continue to develop during the next fifteen years and in an altered tempo for the rest of his life. In this initial phase it was restated and enriched from various perspectives, including *¿Qué es filosofía?* and almost simultaneously his most celebrated book, *The Revolt of the Masses* (1929-30). In his narrative of historical philosophy in *¿Qué es filosofía?* Ortega does indeed explain from a broad perspective his understanding of the philosophic endeavor, but more importantly for our purposes in this writing, this work clarifies the genesis and underpinnings of his own original thought.

No sooner had Ortega assimilated what Germany offered him and immersed himself anew in his Spanish circumstances in 1912 than he began to veer away in dissatisfaction from his German mentors and to develop a species of philosophy that would be authentic in the four paramount senses of the term: universal from a Classical and Western perspective, in conformity to reality, true to the Spanish ethos, and authentically personal, all of which he described as being "at the height of the times." After his experience in Germany and acutely aware of the many shortcomings of his country, he assumed a life-long responsibility for Spain in a variety of ways ranging from university reform and political structure to the Europeanization of Spanish culture to a grand vision of pan-hispanism.

At the same time, Ortega was well aware that not only was there nothing resembling a philosophic tradition in the European mold in Spain but also that the very conditions for its existence were lacking. He was not reluctant to speak of the enormity of the task ahead, as he noted in an early edition of his *Complete Works* (1932): "Thought was my vocation, the urge for clarity about things. Perhaps this congenital fervor made me see very early that one of the characteristic features of my Spanish circumstance was the deficiency of the very thing I had to be because of an inner need. Soon my personal inclination toward the exercise of thought merged with the conviction that it was also service to my country. For this reason, all my work and all my life have been in service to Spain."

But what specific intellectual challenges did Ortega confront upon his return to Madrid and the resumption of his professorial obligations? The first and most pressing was Husserlian phenomenology, particularly Husserl's *Ideen* (1913) with which he was at first infatuated and later disillusioned. Another was the imposing but archaizing presence of Miguel de Unamuno, enemy of modernity and scientific rationality, attitudes the Basque thinker explained in an intoxicating brew of anti-modern defiance and poetic persuasion in *The Tragic Sense of Life* and other writings. There can be no doubt that Unamuno was the only Spanish thinker at the time of sufficient intellectual stature to stand up to Ortega, and even though neither had much to say about the other, save for occasional ill-humored jibes by Unamuno about his younger colleagues, including Ortega, though he called none by name. Nevertheless, their relationship remained outwardly cordial and there was no doubt that at a distance they respected each other. Unamuno was a massive presence: as imposing, archaic, and outdated as a medieval Spanish castle. He had many admirers but was too unique to attract a school of followers.

Julián Marías, the closest of Ortega's many disciples, reveals that Ortega was privately distressed by what he saw as the deliberately irresponsible and anti-intellectual trends in the work of the very formidable Unamuno. It was not a time for timidity. Unamuno had to be challenged, lest his thought sabotage the Europeanizing efforts of Ortega and other thinkers. According to Marías, at one level—there were others—*Meditations on Quixote* was Ortega's passionate reaction to Unamunean irrationalism expressed with monumental passion and persuasion in *The Tragic Sense of Life* published a year earlier.

Ortega and several of his young German classmates regarded Cartesianism as an ingenious and progressive form of philosophy in its day whose advances must be preserved and utilized but which otherwise had run its course and could only be an anachronistic doctrine in the twentieth century. For Ortega there was an additional imperative: the day had passed when Spain could drowse as a European backwater. Europe itself was faltering, and since in Ortega's view Spain was fully European it must therefore share responsibility for its problems. As a consequence of this dual rejection, Ortega was not inclined to take refuge in the safety of traditional doctrines, Germanic, Cartesian, Spanish, or otherwise. Conditions called for new directions in Western thinking to surpass both realism and idealism, between which the philosophical pendulum had swung since the Classical Age. By 1914 he had created the main themes of his new philosophy; by 1929 the doctrine was complete in essence though not finalized in form. Indeed, much of that task would be left to Julián Marías who further systematized the Ortegan doctrines and complemented it with his own empirical theory of life implied but not developed in Ortega's writings. But it should be said here and repeated later: the possibilities and implications of Ortegan thought are only now beginning to be acknowledged and utilized. Hence the premises and purposes of this writing.

Despite the independent pathway Ortega took, he had in common with many thinkers of the early twentieth century, including Unamuno himself, an intuition that idealism—Cartesian or otherwise—was flimsy and archaic and that personal reality was emerging as the paramount theme of the post-modern world. German philosopher Max Scheler (1874-1928), for one, whom Ortega praised and whose influence on his younger contemporary is documented, made human reality paramount by making it problematic. He observes in <u>Vom</u>

Umsturz der Werte [On the Overturn of Value (1919)] that for the first time in the ten-thousand-year recorded history of mankind human reality has become problematical and more to the point that the human being has become indefinable, not a definitive reality at all but a "becoming," a "between," "a self-transcending being."

Scheler's observation suggests two points that have a referential value to this writing: (1) the emerging problematical centrality of human life in modern, or post-modern, European philosophy and science, culminating in what several philosophers and historians perceived in the first instance as a crisis of Western thought and culture (Husserl, Spengler, Ortega), and (2) the perceived linguistic and conceptual inadequacy of traditional philosophic language to describe and treat responsibly the human reality that Scheler describes in his awkward terminology as a "becoming," "a between," "a self-transcending being."

It is possible to take Scheler's remark in an altogether different sense and view man as a transitional reality in the Darwinian paradigm, as a phase in the evolutionary transformation of the human species into a higher and more advanced mammalian being. The theme of evolutionary human transcendence as a species has been treated from religious and humanistic perspectives in such writers as Fr. Teilhard de Chardin in *The Divine Milieu* and Lecomte du Noüy in *Human Destiny* and sensationalized by a variety of racist writers and politicians whose names we shall not mention here. But since Scheler speaks as a philosopher concerned primarily with philosophical concepts of the real, we may assume that he is speaking of human reality as it appears generally in this writing, that is, as advances in intellectual understanding without Darwinian evolutionary or biological overtones.

Here we note that many intellectuals of the modern and contemporary era—Kierkegaard, Unamuno, Marcel, Lewis, Chesterton, Peacocke, Hodgson, Ayala, Barth, among other thinkers—were, and still are in many cases, Christian believers and some, Barth, Chesterton, and Lewis, for example, influential apologists for the Christian faith. But in several we see or sense a divide between intellectual disciplines and faith, as though private beliefs were at a chasmal remove from conventional intellectual and scientific pursuits. This suggests not a failure of faith nor a lapse in doctrinal acumen but a prior lack of a bridging philosophy capable of justifying and accommodating both.

Ortega probably would not quibble with Scheler's bare statement that human life is a "becoming," what one could also describe as "self-becoming," though not self-given. Ortega himself says that life is given us, since we did not give it to ourselves, but it is not given to us in finished form. In this regard, he shares a concept popularized by both atheistic and Christian existentialists such as J-P Sartre and Christian Gabriel Marcel, respectively, that we discover ourselves lost in existence and that it is our responsibility to seek our salvation and forge our life. Hence Sartre's celebrated maxim: "existence precedes essence," which is the commonsense maxim that we must first live in order to become. In this regard, Ortega echoes Scheler by describing mankind as a reality *sui generis,* one of a kind that is ever "coming into being" and thus at once real and partly "unreal." But though accurate, this description does not encapsulate the full human panorama. Life does not simply transmute impersonally into another kind of reality, nor does the human transformation merely happen to us passively without our intervention, as the fatalists and determinists might argue. Western thinkers—though not always Western theologians—have seldom wavered in the conviction that we must make our life or ruin it and thus either create or annihilate our future. Hence the existential turmoil, despair, *Sorge, angst* in the writings of Heidegger, and even themes of justifiable suicide that we come across in existential writers such as Sartre. Nor does the transitional, unreal, and projective dimension of life as Ortega taught mean that it is inherently inferior to other realities or that it necessarily ends in non-being, in the final annihilation of personal life that Bertrand Russell dourly proclaimed and Unamuno majestically dreaded.

By 1914 Ortega had ranged far afield of Husserlian phenomenology. In his stunningly beautiful seminal work, *Meditations on Quixote* he formulated the doctrine he had been searching for since his days in Germany. He summed it up in his celebrated *cogito*: I am I and my circumstance, and if I do not save it I shall not save myself. With this we come the main premise of the Ortegan doctrine: "My life," the life of each person, is the primal or "radical reality" in which all other beings, realities, and things—myself included—appear to me. In my life and your life and the life each person we discover all things real and unreal, present and transcendental, living and lifeless. Things are thus "rooted" in my life. There I discover and deal with them. My life, therefore, is "radical," in the original Latin meaning of "root" and "rootedness." It is the ambit in which all realities known and knowable are grounded and make their appearance circumstantially. My life is where I encounter all realities—and where realities encounter me—including those that transcend me—history, culture, Cosmos, God—and where I discover myself as a living person. (This will be the general theme of Level II of this writing.)

As noted above, as a person I too am "rooted" or "grounded" in "my life," which in turn happens historically and narratively in this world. Being in the Ortegan sense bears a surface resemblance to the Heideggerian concept of *in-der-Welt-sein*, being in the world. But it is vastly more radical and comprehensive. It is not that I simply exist in the world—sticks and stones also exist in it—but rather that the world and its attributions are knowable and experientially present only in my life as I live it. In the Heideggerian paradigm I exist in the physical *umwelt*, the bio-ambient world; in the Ortegan doctrine the world exists for and unto me, and I unto it, and the reciprocal process is what we call living. That I am also bodily installed in the world is a valid subsequent and consequential realization, as we shall see, yet despite its validity still secondary to the primary radical forms of rootedness, or radicalness.

This radical encounter is not only sensorial but also strictly metaphysical. It is not that I apprehend the Cosmos and its contents at an absolute sensorial distance from my life. Instead, my sensory apprehension is the mediating mechanism of reality's immediate, inseparable presence here and now. With this insight, Ortega has reversed and surpassed the Cartesian *Cogito*. The "I," the "ego," alone, spaceless, timeless, and bereft of worldhood is an impossibility. My world and I are indissolubly in mutual reference. It is important to note that 'saving' does not mean in the first instance protecting my circumstantial world from outside forces, though it may come to that, but rather saving it by creatively incorporating it in my life, My circumstances are the only set I have, and if I reject or postpone them as I wait for a utopian world to happen along and unfold before me, then I refuse to live within the only possibilities available to me. In this sense the neglect or rejection of my circumstances is the opposite of saving them. We shall see how the words of his *Cogito* become progressively richer as we proceed. In Part III it will take on further, unexplored dimensions.

The discovery of life in this radical sense is the foundation of Ortega's philosophy, "a tactical turn" in his own words; "an inflection in philosophy," according to Julián Marías. I call it "the tipping point," by which I mean a method of thinking that surpasses the older doctrines that had defined modernity and introduces us a higher level of human understanding, a new style, and with it the possibility of a new age in history, and, so I have come to see, *an enhanced way of reasoning about the possibility of human immortality*. This discovery is not primarily an intellectual deduction even though it is the central premise of Ortegan thought. It is not an undiscovered reality at all to be encoded in the cryptic language so beloved of modern philosophers, not a variant of *Dasein*, not a new tangent of phenomenology, existentialism, idealism, or realism, but instead a reality as close and familiar as our own everyday humanity, because that is precisely what it is: our daily experience of life. For this is what the discovery turns out to be: *human life itself*, and even more personally to the point, *my life. The most elementary fact of life is that I discover myself circumstantially, already and always involved with things, situations, and persons, engaged with and responsive to them—and thus in the largest sense responsible for them—in the comprehensive activity we call living, and more, tasked with the dynamic imperative to go on living*. Therefore, my life is not a status quo that can be defined once and for all, as we might define a physical object, or as we could describe the instincts and features of a biological organism. It is true, as we saw earlier, that there is much in human life that is impersonal and thus obedient to impersonal natural laws and flaws, but in order to understand anything truly human and personal, Ortega reminds us—and here I say again—we must tell a story, that is, relate an episode of our experience and understand its relevance within that experience. Inversely, in order to understand human reality we must hear a human story. Life is understandable biographically, historically, and narratively in obedience to the way this radical mode of reality occurs in time. This insistence on biography over biology is not in the first instance because of the greater intellect or range of human life but because of the way life meshes with time. Our human reality is at once the narrative of who and how we were and who we are and our possibilities of being in the future. We are in time but time is also in us, probably in at least two modes, kaerotic and cosmic, as we shall see in Part III. Human life is also physical being, but not primarily or totally so. We are at once who we are, which includes the lingering, residual reality of "having been," and the potential reality of who we can yet be, of who we are becoming. For this reason, much of our reality is both proto-and pre-reality. In this particular case, Ortegan philosophy converges with, but immediately surpasses, existential philosophy to which several writers erroneously assigned him. Both doctrines hold that in the last analysis our life cannot be subsumed under a biological or genetic classification but must be narrated as a personal biographical reality. But the atheistic strain of existentialism we find in Sartre, or the agnostic version in Heidegger, does not include, and consequently cannot justify, an unimpeachable moral basis in or for life, nor even a rational reason for human life to be in the first place. And least and last of all, no rational reason for believing in the possibility of continuity beyond mortal life, *a possibility that is implicit, as we shall explore, in the Ortegan concept of radical reality.* Hence the old existentialist insistence on the ultimate absurdity of life and the silence or denial when questions of immortality are raised. At best the atheist existentialist can say only that life simply exists, which means, as Sartre logically proclaimed, given the limitations of his doctrine, that man has no ultimate significance and is "a useless passion." And since we live among people supposedly condemned to the same meaningless, absurd fate and who are constant reminders of our own futile human condition, their condition constantly irks and dismays us by mirroring our own finite being. "Hell," Sartre declares, "is others."

With Ortega's transcendent formulation we leave behind all forms of subjectivism, objectivism, idealism, and realism of older philosophies. My life is not primarily a thing, object, element, or biological reality that may be measured, weighed, or described in metric, molecular, or chemical terms, as the realists would tell us. Nor is it merely fiction, abstraction, idea, concept, or thought, as the idealists would argue. My life is manifestly real, but world-laden and world-responsible, a reality unlike any of those just mentioned. Phenomenologically, we perceive its effects and experience its presence, pressures, and movements in ourselves and others. Life is an ever-emerging reality. We cannot confine it to a definition; it is undefined, unconfined, and characterized by its unbounded, universal scope. It consists not only in its present state of being but also, and arguably more so, in its possible states of being. We can only accompany it narratively and historically, always respecting its protean, creative potentialities. This means that human life is an "eventual" reality in two senses: first, because it happens eventfully as discrete moments and episodes or chapters, and second, because it is futuristic, consisting in part of who a person may become, that is, eventually—and eventfully—become. And apparently physically ceases to be. Life, the great mystery, ends in death, no less a mystery, for as Shakespeare reminds us, from its "bourne no traveller returns." We abide in the interval, to forge or falsify our life. In either case, I discover my life as a projective, futuristic endeavor that I must complete, or fail to complete. In order to do either, I must reach out to my circumstances for the resources needed to become who I strive to be, that is, to act out my drama, to write my story, or to compose the melody of my life. Or alternatively, to fail to do so. We could say that my life resembles a literary genre or musical compositions and that I am responsible for completing the work. I may opt to compose as little and poorly as possible, for declining to choose is also a choice. We soon perceive the choices a person has made and in doing so reveal the caliber of our own. For unless we have numbed our senses with unwise options we cannot fail to feel the human loss and diminished main that the poet Donne spoke of.

Within a certain range, these life choices are mine to make. But not entirely: as far as I know, I did not choose to be born into my family, culture, time, and circumstance. Nor can I disregard the inexplicable vocational calling that certain people sense must take precedence over all other possibilities. To ignore the call is to make a tragedy of life, even though the calling itself may involve tragedy of a different sort. Otherwise what most of us may choose and must is to make the best or worst of life with the circumstantial odds that aid or oppose me. Folk wisdom has ever taught as much. But my choices are historically and circumstantially limited. I cannot realistically aspire to be a medieval knight, an Egyptian pharaoh, or time traveler, because those possibilities are not available to me. Thus contrary to a favorite American fable that we can be anything we strive to become, our options are limited by our circumstances. Otherwise, they would not be options and require no hope and resolution but mere decisions about our limitless possibilities.

The first step in taking intellectual possession of a reality is to name it. What we cannot say, we do not fully possess. For this reason, the radical concepts of Ortegan philosophy required a revision of language. The philosophic lexicon at his disposal as he was formulating his philosophy was derived from the intellectual conventions more or less shared and translated by all the Western countries but ill-suited for his new doctrine. Not even Ortega, master writer and orator that he was, could completely overcome the deeply embedded assumptions inherent in the older terminology. His linguistic innovations were ingenious and several of them soon made their way into the popular language—his particular use of *"circumstance"* for example and the popularity of his *cogito—I am I and my circumstance*. Yet misunderstandings lingered, in some cases with malice aforethought and a deliberate will to sabotage his philosophy. His philosophy was a new wine, but there were those who insisted—and still insist—on pouring it into old wineskins.

Furthermore, there was, or would be within a generational span, another popular hypothesis, itself philosophic, regarding the fundamental fidelity of language. Can we really trust language to describe what we mean to say? Ludwig Wittgenstein (1889-1951) and his French and Anglo-American followers made linguistic analysis an important but restricted branch of philosophy. Contemporary philosophers of language atomize and deconstruct conventional language—and many other things besides—raising doubts about whether words could be trusted to convey truth at all in any absolute sense, and generally concluding that they cannot be fully or naively counted on to do so. At bottom, linguistic deconstruction is suited to the skeptical mind. Conversely, words can be coaxed or coerced into admitting other meanings. Language conceals as much as it reveals. Scheler pointed to the problem in his day and Heidegger struggled with linguistic elusiveness as he explored the deep implications of *existenz* and *Dasein*.

At the other end of the spectrum, Ortega addressed the lack of an established philosophical idiom and lexicon in Spain from a very different vantage point. Instead of raising doubts about the reliability of all language and justifying a radical skepticism regarding all claims to truth, he resorted to a new metaphorical system to dramatize his concepts. Although he was disappointed at times by the inability of his readers to understand his method and intent, he had no doubts about his verbal wizardry or the efficacy of language to express truth. After all, it has an immemorial history of reasonable success in doing so. Otherwise, there would be no philosophical tradition to start with, nor any intellectual heritage to deconstruct.

As the master metaphysician of Spain, Ortega kept in mind something that the Northern European and American deconstructionists generally overlook: that in order to convey truth to people—particularly Mediterranean people—he must first seduce them with verbal beauty. Language is much more than sounds and signifiers. Words come haloed with beauty and euphonic rhythm or diminished by cacophonous disharmonies. Truth poorly told might do for Anglo-Germanic peoples with a modern tradition of material pragmatism and simplified theology, but not for Mediterranean audiences for whom truth and aesthetics have been euphonically and visually inseparable in art and liturgy for ages.

Ortega's systematic use of metaphor is in some respects nearly as remarkable as his metaphysical discoveries, though often poorly understood and dismissed as an impressive but unteachable personal method. It is true that his efforts do not easily translate into other languages. Like Heidegger whose language stoutly resists translation into other tongues, Ortega's genius, though often impressive in other languages, also appears too baroque for easy translation. The words usually correspond but the spirit is often diminished.

But we are getting a bit ahead of ourselves in one way and behind in another. Now it is proper to ask how Ortega derived his view of human life and how does it differ from conclusions that Descartes and Leibniz reached in early modernity and Husserl in its latter stages? In this circularity we employ what Ortega called "the Jericho Method." It is the strategy harking back to the ancient Hebrews of circling the strategic target under siege, confronting it from various perspectives until it yields to the final assault. Philosophy has its analogies to military strategy.

Curiously enough, the "discovery" of human life as the "radical reality" occurred in the same historical period during which human life had been reduced in, if not entirely divested of, its sacral transcendence, as we saw in the introduction. Defying the rip tides of conventional philosophy, Ortega refused to trivialize human life in the existentialist manner or to render undue reverence to the archaic past with Unamuno and other anti-modern thinkers. Instead he set out to reenchant the world, which for him meant to offer a new and more optimistic metaphysics—life as the radical reality—coupled with a prideful vision of the possibilities of European and Western civilization. And not least, to do so in language that would seduce the spirit and stroke the intellect. I repeat that Ortega's mastery of the Western philosophic tradition and language may cause us to forget that he is heir to no long tradition in his own country. But this is all the more reason to underscore the equally significant fact that this cultural lack in his own country freed him from national limitations and allowed him to migrate to the historical center of the Western tradition. In this sense, it can be argued that by necessity Ortega was the most "Western" thinker of his time. Heidegger could be fully German in his philosophy, as Comte could be entirely French in his. But Ortega had to work outside nationalistic modes to construct a doctrine from a much wider perspective. Not that this implied that Spain ceased to matter in Ortega's expanded European context. He thought of Spain as a virginal land ready to absorb and enrich the Western ethos: "Europe, tired in France, exhausted in Germany, weak in England, will have a second youth under our land's powerful sun." Once again, he proved to be a prophet. Although it is not generally known, at the moment thanks largely to Ortega and Julián Marías, Spain enjoys probably the most vigorous youthful philosophical movement in the Western world.

Ortega foresaw the exhaustion of the "meta-narratives,"

which Joseph Campbell and others refer to later as the recurring foundational "myths" of Western civilization. More compassionate but even bleaker in his outlook than Sartre and Spengler, Bertrand Russell thought that humanity's common historical hopes, to say nothing of its transcendent beliefs, were pathetic whispers lost in the mindless, indifferent Cosmos. Ortega was far from such gloom about the human condition. He sought to awaken his readers to the beauty and majesty of reality, human reality most of all. The world for him is marvelous, and everywhere so: "There is nothing in the orb through which some divine nerve does not pass."

In his preference for seductive, lyrical phrasing, Ortega stands in contrast to Heidegger and many of his philosophic counterparts for whom murky depth was the mark of deep insights. And this conviction convinced the rest of us. Today we take easy language to mean empty thought. Ortega himself plunged into the philosophic depths, and every page of his writings bulges with a wealth of concepts perhaps unequaled by any other modern thinker. But he also had the good sense and authorial courtesy to bring his discoveries back up to the surface, as a pearl diver brings the pearls from the marine depths, for all to see and admire. In this sense, Ortega declared that philosophy must be an exercise in "superficiality" if it is to accomplish its clarifying purpose. Husserl himself said that confusion exists in the depths and that clarity and precision are surface dimensions. Consequently, *Meditations on Quixote* is diaphanous in its light and clarity, emitting beams of significance radiating in all directions. Reminiscent of the Platonic texts, Ortegan thought is pure philosophy that reads like pure poetry.

Near the beginning of the *Meditations* he pays tribute to

Spinoza's "intellectual love" and then affirming that "philosophy is the general science of love," Ortega begins to display the doctrinal treasures brought up from the philosophical depths: insights into surface and depth; the theory of the "radical reality" of life as the organizing principle of circumstance, vital reason, the idea of living as the most basic form of reasoning, and almost unnoticed, the mystery of space and distance, about which I shall add comments later in this writing.

Nevertheless, it is obvious that non-Ortegan philosophy—pre-Ortegan in its assumptions, levels and methods—continues to slog along with its inelegant language. Murky language is so widespread and obligatory in contemporary thought that it has all but removed most forms of modern philosophy from public awareness and consigned it to intellectual specialists who teach and write about such matters, and with few exceptions, only for one another. Gone for good, it seems, are the heady days of earlier centuries when Descartes, Voltaire, Diderot, Locke, Paine, and Rousseau made their appeal more or less directly to receptive, appreciative masses. And apparently enjoyed themselves in the process. It may have been the last time before Ortega that philosophers had fun. Beginning with Kant generations of glumness unrelieved by intellectual clarity lay ahead.

Little has changed. Philosophy in our day is for the most part an intramural code among professional philosophers, or better said perhaps, professors of philosophy, for the two camps often differ. Not that it is divinely ordained that philosophy be condemned forever to pedestrian language. As we see in ¿Qué es filosofía?, Ortega set out to re-enchant philosophy by investing it with visions of heroic philosophic freedom and sensations of beauty. He was determined to wean it away from the Cartesian-dependent Husserlian idealism and Teutonic heaviness, and with lyrical language to permeate it with the enthusiastic *élan* that he had not found in Germany. By doing so, he invited the public to gather in the thronging marketplace of ideas. And, remarkably, for a time he succeeded.

Despite Ortega's descriptive artistry, however, it took all his skill to make his audiences and readers understand the concept of "radical reality" and its significance. Even though man is an immemorial theme of experience and art, the subject of human life took its time in becoming a major concern of modern philosophy. Ortega sought to remedy the deficiency in several ways in his writings, including a modification of philosophic genres, the introduction of new terminology often extracted but elevated from common speech, and, as noted, his free use of metaphor which some have scorned for being more akin to poetic lyricism than modern philosophy. And they were right, for Ortega was not interested in producing more "modern" philosophy but instead in introducing an entirely new way of philosophizing.

It is interesting to note that like the dual-faced god Janus, Spain's two leading philosophers in the early decades of the twentieth century had diametrically opposing perspectives. Whereas Unamuno looked back to traditional Spain, Ortega looked forward to a renewed Spanish presence in Western civilization. The lack of an established philosophic tradition in Spain paradoxically worked to Ortega's advantage. As we saw earlier, he was not bound by the older modes, but his disadvantage was the fact that his professional public was slow to understand anything else. Those reduced to imitation are also confined to arch-conservatism. In his own way and in a much deeper sense than Unamuno, Ortega was a philosophical pioneer whose revolutionary teachings took their time to ripen and bear fruit. And the main harvest is yet to come. His was a role he assumed not out of simple dissidence but one thrust upon him by the Spanish and European circumstances in which it was his destiny to be born. He wrote landmark books, made the case for his thought journalistically when necessary and convenient, and when other venues were lacking, as in the case of *¿Qué es filosofía?*, took his case directly to the public. But I repeat that the older modes, genres, and presuppositions had a tenacious grip on intellectuals, who seemed to have more problems understanding Ortega than the general public who read his works and listened to him without the intellectually crippling presuppositions of the sophisticates.

4. Beyond Realism and Idealism

The physical surroundings in which Ortega delivered the eleven lectures of *¿Qué es filosofía?* were as unusual as they were challenging. The audience soon overflowed Cinema Rex, prompting Ortega to move the course to the larger Beatriz Theater to accommodate the growing numbers. It was the first course on pure philosophy outside a university setting and before the most heterogeneous audience imaginable. It was made up not only of "professionals," that is, students of philosophy and dilettantes of intellectual pleasures, but also and in greater numbers by people unversed in philosophy and whose interest in such themes no one would have suspected. Moreover, the extensive themes grew more complex with each lecture as step by step, component by component, Ortega explained not only the systematic structure of his philosophy but also the variations of the philosophical enterprise over the centuries. Nevertheless, the audience continued to swell until the end of the course.

Here we take another look at a common criticism of Ortega: that for all his rhetorical brilliance he did not develop a coherent "systematic" philosophy, but instead scattered suggestive and disjunctive nuggets of his thought throughout his works and borrowed others from German sources. In order to counter these dismissive claims, it seems to me that we need only point out that while Ortega always acknowledged his German teachers and contemporaries and read their works voraciously, as he did almost every major writer, ancient or modern, there is nothing one can point to in Germany that comes close to the philosophy of radical reality that Ortega developed in Spain. The nearest any German thinker came to Ortega—or vice versa—may have been the little-known nineteenth-century historian-philosopher Wilhelm Dilthey (1833-1911). Dilthey was obsessed with the historicity of human life and the idea that much of it predates us, a concept briefly mentioned earlier. But as Ortega noted in a long essay, *Guillermo Dilthey y la idea de la vida* [Wilhelm Dilthey and the Idea of Life], Dilthey's intuition was superior to his doctrine. He remained stuck midway through his idea and was never able to explain its full implications, even though he labored to do so for nearly thirty years following the publication of his most important work, *Introduction to the Sciences of the Spirit* (1883). Dilthey's work attracted little attention in Germany, much more in Spain where Ortega saw to it that his works were translated and commented.

Ortega returned to Spain the first time (1907) grateful to his German mentors but dissatisfied with the neo-Kantian thought then prevalent in Germany, and after his second sojourn in Germany (1911) even more dissatisfied with the direction phenomenologist Husserl was taking. Husserl insisted for purposes of analysis on the "suspension" or *epoché*, of experience, a tactic that Ortega described as an impossibility. Life does not stop for our leisurely analysis, he argued, but continues dramatically without pause, and we must take it in its continuous flood. This objection together with his disapproval of Husserl's announced "return" to Descartes were among the factors that prompted Ortega and several other followers to break with their mentor. In Ortega's case, it freed him to develop a doctrine already an intuition that was beginning to take shape as an intuition. Ortega wrote after his years in Germany that he found admirable teachers and a philosophic tradition second to none in German universities; what he did not find there was a viable philosophy. Indeed, Ortega faulted his German mentors for being insufficiently "scrupulous" and for their excessive zeal to be right.

For a brief time in 1912-13 it did appear, however, that Husserlian phenomenology might turn out to be the philosophic meat that he and other young philosophers of his generation were hungry for. But he was soon disappointed when in the end Husserl himself confessed that he could not escape the gravitational pull of Cartesianism, which for Ortega and other the young German philosophers, including Heidegger, was a step backward into a once fertile but now outdated idealism. Rather than the philosophy he sought, phenomenology was "a stroke of good luck" that made clear to Ortega what his philosophy could not be.

The concept of philosophic system, as Ortega understood it

and as we examined briefly in an earlier context, may be taken in two different and usually conflicted ways. For Ortega, it is unnecessary to add a system to authentic philosophy, in his case the philosophy of human life as the fundamental or "radical" reality. It is worth emphasizing now what we mentioned earlier: *by its nature his philosophy is already systematic because of its "radicality."* Life is the biographical, circumstantial system that supports and orders all other human systems, as the surface must conform to the subsoil in order to be a surface in the first place. It does not lend itself to secondary forms but always retains its foundational integrity. It turns out that the debate over "system" in Ortegan philosophy involves not only the dichotomy of inherent and superimposed systems but also a matching confusion between system and genre. By Ortega's time it was generally assumed, though unjustifiably so, that philosophy must conform to the patterns established in 19th century Germany. But it had appeared in other forms in different eras: the medieval discourse consisting of the interplaying dialectic of thesis and antithesis, Plato's poetic prose, to mention only two examples. These were different modes for different minds and times. The Platonic texts, for example, bear little resemblance to the conventional "systems" of nineteenth-century thinkers. Textual form is, or should be, the obedient servant, just as philosophical content, that is to say, reality itself is the informing master. To reverse the order is to condemn philosophy to greater or lesser degrees of scholasticism. So-called "Medieval philosophy," for example, was scholastic for the simple reason that it was not philosophy in a pure sense but rather a system borrowed from Classical Aristotelianism and imposed on a later age. Aristotle was the philosopher, not primarily St. Thomas

Aquinas and the other Medieval Masters who taught and applied it.

As Ortega saw it, therefore, philosophic system is inherent, inevitable, and ineradicable so long as it centers on the organizing, systematic reality of human life. But let me caution anew that this assertion is easily misunderstood and indeed commonly has been so misconstrued. Even though the philosophy of radical reality is structured on human life, specifically "my life," the life of each person, it must not be taken in a rigid, abstract sense. The freedom that informs life and makes history possible in the first place is pliable to our thoughts about it. It gracefully adapts to, and embraces, history and art, love and biography, psychology and sociology, epistemology, metaphysics, aesthetics, science and theology. It does not disdain fiction and poetry, and the most modest anecdotal human fact can find accommodation within it. With Ortega philosophy begins once again to veer in step with Cicero's ancient claim that "philosophy is the art of life" and no less with Terence's celebrated proclamation: "I am a man; nothing human is alien to me." This is not to say that Ortega himself covered the full range of this humane philosophy. For instance, he had little to say about mortality and theological matters, and what he did say was characteristically guarded, one is tempted to say tentative and almost tepid in tone. He said very little publicly, for example, even about his father's death. Why so? There are several possible reasons, or better, conjectures. Above all, Ortega set out to clarify and explain. But his informing concern was the radical reality of life, less about the uncertainties of death and immortality. Julián Marías offers the plausible explanation that Ortega chose not to encroach on a theme which Unamuno had treated passionately and persistently, particularly in *The Tragic Sense of Life* and literarily in *San Manuel Bueno, Mártir*. In his own work in which he extends and deepens the philosophy of radical reality, Marías himself did not hesitate to apply this way of thinking to transcendent dimensions of human life and to speculations about immortality. For Marías the very logic of radical reality urged him to consider the continuity of life. And we are even more attuned to that theme in this writing.

Ortega covers an immense philosophical territory in these lectures, which is a primary indication that the work is not a hastily erected doctrinal firewall against Heideggerian ideas, as Orringer, Ouimette, and other critics have claimed. In fact, no such tactic is mentioned at all. Instead, Ortega answers the question of what philosophy is by patiently retracing its history and permutations from ancient to modern times. He does so as a comprehensive survey, not as an annotated account of each phase and period of philosophy. This approach is understandable given his heterodox audience, but it also shows his unpressured patience in the task.

Nevertheless, this historical survey is not incidental to the meaning of philosophy, as he understood it. The fact that human life is invested with freedom and therefore has—and is—a history and that it is radical in the first instance because it is a human reality, that is, a personal reality in time, means that philosophy, as the art of life, must also be historical. In this sense, the sense of historical reason, the history of philosophy reveals itself to be identical to philosophy itself.

As for the circumstances under which Ortega delivered these lectures, it is important to point out the inconveniences he faced, some of which were mentioned at the beginning of these commentaries: an unusually large and diverse public, wary officialdom, the exotic setting outside the university walls—*extramuros*—which deprived the speaker of familiar university surroundings and supports—a situation that could expose him to potentially disruptive influences and unsympathetic scrutiny—and the length and complexity of the lessons, which required rigorous doctrinal discipline and not only an uncommon mastery of content but also, and not least, sustained rhetorical power and stamina. Most of all, he risked losing before an untutored audience the normal respect for the *verba magistri*, the words of the teacher, which usually confers an automatic degree of professorial authority in a university classroom.

At the same time, however, can we not say that Ortega was in his ideal element in such a setting? Where better for one keenly aware of the dramatic cast of philosophy than by ironic happenstance to be on a theatrical stage? What public better suited to his talents and purposes than a heterodox audience, a veritable microcosm of the Spanish populace, assembled so as to be mesmerized and initiated by the master metaphysician into the great philosophical drama of human life? We have seen how Ortega thought of philosophy as a heroic voyage into the unknown. He often uses nautical terms and calls man a *náufrago*, a shipwrecked sailor, who thrown into the flotsam of human calamity must sink to his doom or swim for a distant shore. For him, philosophy was an exercise in high drama in which mental dexterity and sportive challenge had their part: It was the reenactment of enlightened man imposing his will on the unruly world. It was the pursuit of the elusive unicorn; clever Theseus defeating the monstrous Minotaur, Odysseus outwitting hideous Polyphemus, Perseus slaying the dreadful Gorgon, metaphors all of man pitting his wits against the dark forces of worldly torpor and ignorance. Nor does Ortega pause to consolidate his victories or organize the strongholds he has won. He races on across the philosophical landscape, conquering all in his pathway with tactical brilliance and overwhelming intellectual power and passion. Gordian knots do not faze him; they simply unravel under his seductive dialectical caress. Then like a new Alexander, as philosopher Rafael Hidalgo describes him, he is off to new conquests, but in the enigmatic West, not the mysterious East. He sees all at a glance and strikes unerringly at strategic points. His method is not a ponderous army of concepts laying lengthy siege to problems but can be compared to deftly executed cavalry thrusts that confuse and rout resistance. It is a triumph of intellectual grace over dug-in dogma. If the Ortegan attitude could be symbolized artistically, it might well be Velásquez's *Rendición de Breda* [Surrender of Breda] with its dramatic balance of gallantry, heroism, generosity, and nobility.

Ortega was reaching the peak of his powers in those early months of 1929. If *Meditaciones del Quijote* was his most poetic work, and *La rebelión de las masas* his most dramatic, *What Is Philosophy?* was perhaps his most unorthodox philosophical venture. The time had come to launch his philosophy in its full compelling significance before the widest public available. The lectures exude his confidence, his assurance, that he has escaped the downward gravitational pull of Cartesian subjectivism, its descendant phenomenology, and no less, what Ortega often referred to as the "bourgeois realism" of the positivists and pragmatists, on which so much of modernity was founded. He is in prime form, holding nothing back; each lesson deepens and broadens the theme of the new vision of the philosophic enterprise. And his audience stays with him, swelling its ranks, warming to the task, caught up in the excitement, if not yet the mastery of the new themes. Still, Ortega is archly respectful and does not plunge heedlessly ahead. Always mindful of his audience, he offers an early cautionary note: "There lies before us a new life . . . I am not disposed to say all I see. It would be to no avail, frightening without convincing, and it would frighten because it would not be understood, better said, because it would be misunderstood."

But let us pause before the finale and retrace a few steps to make other linkages between *What Is Philosophy?* and *Meditations on Quixote.* We begin by returning to the heart of Ortegan philosophy and his *cogito*: "I am I and my circumstance, and if I do not save it I shall not save myself." This is gorgeous language, beautifully concise, but precisely what does it mean, particularly in light of *What Is Philosophy?* Fifteen years later with a bow to Descartes, Ortega now declares to his audience: "We need, therefore, to correct the point of departure of philosophy. The radical datum of the Universe is not simply that thought exists or I exist as a thinking being—but rather if thought exists then *ipso facto*, there exists the I who thinks, and the world in which I think—and the one exists with the other without any possible separation. But alone neither I nor the world is a substantial being. Instead we are, we exist, only in active correlation: I am one who sees the world and the world is what is seen by me. I am for the world and the world is for me. If there were no things to see, think, or imagine, then I would not see, think, or imagine—that is to say, I would not be."

The nucleus of the Ortegan doctrine and the intense intellectual concentration that allows him to escape Cartesian-

Husserlian subjectivity was already implied in his famous maxim of 1914. But here the reasoning is extended. Ortega finds no reason to deny that Descartes was on solid ground in asserting that thinking is, or can be, the proof of "my" existence, *provided the formula for "my" existence is complete.* And the completion is this: if I see, think, or imagine, I can only do so if there is *something* to see, think, or imagine. I am aware of myself only insofar as I am appositionally aware of objects and other beings that are not I. Descartes stopped short: I think, as he reasoned, *but I think only if there are things to think about.* The most fundamental fact of life, therefore, is not my solitary existence but rather my circumstantial coexistence with the world and especially the people in it. In reality neither Descartes nor Husserl is discredited by the Ortegan dialectic. They are his starting point on the road to radical reality. Their contributions are preserved in an expanded paradigm. In this sense Ortega did indeed continue to be indebted to Descartes and Husserl as well as to many other thinkers, but his debt should not be taken, as too often it seems to be, as a disqualification of his own contributions to philosophy that flesh out and transcend modern idealism in the Cartesian and Husserlian modes. His intuition was the heart of the matter, the inspiration for a new form and level of philosophizing that reunites the world and me.

It should be noted in this context that "my" relationship with the world, my circumstantial coexistence, has multiple moral and ethical dimensions. My inseparability from the world signifies more than the bare words declare. I cannot save myself by ignoring or betraying the world, things, and other persons, for all are a part of my circumstance, all a part of my reality. Hence the second part of the Ortegan *Cogito*: "…if I do not save it, I do not save myself." The structure and the moral injunction are firm and imperative, and if, as Ortega writes in the *Meditations*, everything, and everyone, carries within the possibility of a plenitude, it means also that each one also bears within the disquieting possibility of frustration and failure.

Therefore, we cannot live in what the old Romantics would call "splendid isolation." Only the memories, technics, religion, and moral lessons of old Europe kept Robinson Crusoe from becoming a bestial degenerate. He was alone but not isolated from humanity. As Scheler noted, without the resistance of things and others, the ego would tend to expand to monstrous proportions, as it does frequently with despots whose desires range unchecked. The first part of the Ortegan *Cogito* appears to be the passive status of life as I discover it, but this impression is dispelled by the second half, which is active and executive: I must reach out to my circumstances in salvific gestures, saving them and myself as an inseparable tandem. The world and I constitute a sum of our mutual possibilities.

Here—it is now May of 1929—Ortega begins his final ascent to liberating, transcendent conclusions: the world offers things for me to see; I could not see if there were nothing to see, nor could I know without an appositional relationship with things outside my mind; there can be no subject without objects. Things and I, others and I, the world and I, are in reciprocal relationships, each co-dependent on, and co-implicated—and thus complicated by—the other. My being begins not with an initial embrace of the Cosmos at large—too vast and vague as a first effort—but with my immediate circumstances near at hand. In order to live at all, I must do so relationally with the immediate. My subjectivity depends on the objective presence of things and persons without any possible separation. Subjects and objects are hypothetical in separation; only in union they are realized and completed. I am aware of myself only by becoming aware of objects that are not I but correlational to me. Therefore, the most fundamental fact is not my singular existence deriving from my thinking but rather my coexistence, my life, with the world in order to think at all. I coexist and live with, and by means of, the components of my circumstance. I think them, suffer them, use them, understand them, oppose them, and perhaps love them. The fuller meaning of his 1914 cogito now becomes apparent and revelatory. The relationship is sealed, and we can say with its full range of meaning: I am I and my circumstance, and if I do not save it, I shall not save myself.

At the end of this long dialectical road, which we have so briefly trodden here, with the exuberance that was typical of his thinking at this moment of his life, Ortega describes the euphoric freedom: "We are outside the confines of the ego, the sealed room of the sick, a room of mirrors that despairingly reflected back to us our own profile. We are outside, in the fresh air, our lungs again open to the cosmic oxygen, our wings ready for flight, and our hearts directing us to that which is lovely."

It was indeed a moment of euphoria, but like all human euphoria it was not destined to last. The philosophical community little heeded and most soon forgot Ortega's dramatic gambit. *What Is Philosophy?* for example, long remained only marginally available in Spain and did not appear in English until 1960, five years after Ortega's death when his image had largely disappeared from public awareness. Few of his works appeared in French, more in English and German. Long before his passing his personal and professional life was in considerable disarray.

At the height of his power and influence in 1936 he was obliged to go into exile, and when he returned to Spain in 1945-46 he was more of a historical curiosity than a public voice of intellectual authority. He had lost a decade of Spanish life and, as Julián Marías would note, a step along with it. Still, there would be other important achievements: the collaborative Institute of Humanities (1948-50) with Marías, honors and recognition abroad, including North America, important writings that reestablished his standing in Spain and Latin America. But the early exuberance was diminished and he was frequently despondent. Announced works were not completed. He was not as prescient and hopeful as before. His early patriotic socialism was now far behind him. He foresaw only a dark age of international socialistic despotism looming in the future. Health problems slowed him, and he died October 18, 1955.

What then can one say of Ortega in summary? Perhaps only this: despite an array of obstacles, his philosophy and its potential survive, awaiting those with the determination, creativity, and generosity of mind and spirit to develop it and put it to good use. In this writer's opinion, he originated the most advanced philosophy since Descartes and Kant. Dozens of pathways beckon to us in his thought. And not everybody forgot his teachings. Julian Marias, for example, took it to a higher level, and specialists in many fields benefited from his insights.

What Julián Marías describes as "page quality" is probably nowhere richer in modern thought than in Ortega, at least none I know of. Practically every page is replete with philosophic nuggets that molded and shaped could fill whole books. The exuberant Ortega at the height of his intellectual and lyrical power is almost irresistible. Ideas pour from his writings and lectures as water gushes full force from an open hydrant. He offers no neutral middle ground to those who read him, but almost always polarizes them instead into two camps: those who laud and those who loathe his genius. His impact on the Spanish language was nearly as divisive, especially during his prime years. Those who read him displayed an enhanced gracefulness of style, while those ignorant of his work often retained the stilted formalism of older Spanish. But then as now there are dangers for those who wander too close to his brilliance and try to soar higher stylistically than their talent allows, like Icarus who flew too close to the sun and got his makeshift feathers disastrously scorched. As a stylist, Ortega is not for the timid. In most cases, his style is more to be admired than imitated. Oddly enough, however, Ortega was also a philosophical popularizer. He introduced philosophy to several generations of non-specialists and brought it back to the public arena, as ages earlier Socrates popularized his teaching to the public hum of the Athenian *Agora*.

It is easy to understand why earnest scholars of his work have labeled Ortega in so many conflicting ways and why it is hard for anyone to resist doing so. He was awash with talents and matching complexity. If one searches for them within his life and writings there may be found the proofs of his liberalism and conservatism, his openness to other thinkers and his own originality. He can be categorized at once as a man of the privileged and the populace, which caused him to be generally distrusted by politicians of all stripes, though at one time he was himself a politician. In time he outgrew all political labels. Theologians attacked him relentlessly, though he was never anticlerical and publicly ignored the assaults. He spoke little of his religious beliefs but confided as he neared death that he had always been in God's hands. He was distrusted and opposed by the Franco dictatorship, the Church hierarchy, the Right, the Left, and the University. But he stayed the course and almost singlehandedly established a vibrant philosophic tradition in Spain and did more to bring his country into the European community than the entire Generation of 1898. Excellence marked nearly all his many efforts. He was a man in control of himself, given to mirth and melancholy but often stricken with illness. Ortega was alternately honored and exiled, praised and slandered. Like many Spaniards of his time, he was obliged, or felt obliged, to do too much, perhaps to write too much. Great gifts often short circuit into eccentricities. This was not true of Ortega; he knew who he was and what he could do and consequently felt no need for false modesty or pretenses, least of all vain self-promotion. He had many hopes, but he was no airy optimist. He wrote that humanity was sliding into another of its periodic valleys of stupidity, and the maelstrom of the Spanish Civil War and World War II rendered his words prophetic. He never knew the sheltered world of the godlike nineteenth-century German professor or the Oxford don trailing honors behind ivied walls. The granite-hard world of Spain was ever very much with him and as often officially against him. Only average citizens admired him as a Spanish icon and unfailingly responded to him when they had the chance. Like other Spaniards over the ages, including Cervantes, he wrote amid oppositions that would have crushed a weaker person. But through it all and by all accounts, he did so with princely grace. In him it may be said that Buffon's dictum came true: style was the man.

Ortega did what he could, but it was not enough. No individual life is ever enough. Those who follow the great either elevate their legacy to fullness or consign it to failure. The past belongs less to those who live it than to us who inherit it. Ortega was, I repeat my conviction, the foremost Western thinker of the modern centuries, which, if true, places on us who call ourselves Westerners a responsibility as heirs of his legacy and guardians of his insights. If he had a personal credo, it would be Goethe's verse that he often cited: "I am of those who from the darkness aspire to the light."

Part II:

The Structure of Mortal Life

5. Saving the Circumstances

In the second part of his celebrated *Cogito* Ortega said in reference to circumstance that "if I do not save it, I shall not save myself." For his young disciple Julián Marías the imperative became personal in two ways. First, theoretical, because he was convinced that Ortega was right, and second, because his own circumstances were highly problematic at the end of the Spanish Civil War in 1939. I have summarized the philosophical story of Ortega; now it becomes my task and privilege to attempt the same for Marías.

Marías calls Ortega the "discoverer" a new continent of philosophy, but it is fair to say that at first neither Ortega nor anyone else knew exactly what to make of the unexplored territory. As a result, there was much misunderstanding about his discovery. It was left to Marías to trace its coordinates and show us how to apply Ortega's concept of "radical reality" and its instrumentality of historical or narrative reason to actual history and concrete human circumstance. He did so impressively in several works, especially in his bestselling book [*España inteligible* (1985)]; in English, [*Understanding Spain* (1989)], something Ortega himself had not done in his own writings. This application of historical reason to the specific history of Spain is based on principles that Marías explained in *Metaphysical Anthropology* (1970).

Marías describes his philosophical relationship to Ortega as "filial," that is, inexplicable without him but irreducible to him.

Theirs was an intellectual symbiosis unparalleled, as far as I know, in modern philosophy, and since it involved thinkers with different temperaments but similar creative gifts, perhaps without parallel in the history of Western thought. Philosophy is a lonely endeavor, but at its best it is shared loneliness, not mere isolation. Sycophantic allegiance of lesser minds to leading thinkers is common. But vanity often marks those of middling talents, impelling them to separate from their masters and establish their own intellectual hegemony, sometimes to their credit, as often to their disadvantage. In any case, Marías, like Ortega, was above such tactics. Their pact of loyal friendship and collaboration was never broken but instead deepened with the years, resulting in a superior level of thinking that brought out the best in both philosophers. It serves no purpose to speculate unduly about hypotheticals, but it is possible that alone neither could have done what they achieved in collaboration, particularly in the case of Marías. In ancient Chinese culture the achievements of the child elevated the father and ancestors to greater dignity. Ortega's case is similar; were it not for Marías he might have remained a marginal footnote in the history of philosophy. As it is, their dual philosophy continues to expand and attract. In fact, in recent years the "elder" trails the "younger"; Marías grows in popularity, but Ortega's prestige necessarily resurges in the process. Which is the greater thinker? I cannot make a graduated distinction between two very different but very gifted philosophers. And I have no reason to try.

Their association, but naturally not yet their collaboration, began when Marías (1914-2005) had the good fortune to study under Ortega at the University of Madrid (1932-36), but the bad luck to earn his undergraduate degree on the eve of the Spanish

Civil War (1936-39). The first experience turned him definitively toward philosophy; the second would close all official doors to him in Spain.

He despised a great many things the Spanish Republic tolerated but supported it as the lesser of evils because of its electoral legitimacy. Later he described the war as a conflict that neither belligerent deserved to win. As a radio broadcaster in the French language during the war, Marías took consolation in the fact that he was not responsible for anyone's death. As the war was ending in 1939 he was denounced by an envious classmate—once his closest friend—and spent three months in prison. Upon his provisional release, he emerged without professional prospects. Livelihood was a pressing concern. He took stock of his limited prospects: "I could not be a professor, a deep and undeniable calling, in the official Spanish institutions. I could perhaps write essays in the few journals that could accept a person in my situation. Newspapers were inaccessible to me and remained so for a dozen years, until 1951. What was left? My philosophic vocation was imperative, and no less so was my calling to be a writer. The only authentic recourse was to write books of philosophy."

Circumstances pushed him to the verge of penury, but his intelligence and knowledge were uncommonly vast. Encouraged by his classmate Dolores Franco—later his wife—Marías began writing an ambitious *Historia de la Filosofía* (History of Philosophy). For political reasons the University withheld his doctorate until 1951, even though his doctoral dissertation, *La filosofía del Padre Gratry* (The Philosophy of Father Gratry) was acclaimed for its quality and published as a book in 1941. But there was no doubt about the success of his *History*, published that same year. From exile in Buenos Aires and without having seen the manuscript, Ortega approved its publication by his family press *Revista de Occidente*. The three thousand copies of the first edition reportedly sold out in three days, and dozens of editions and printings followed, and continue to this day. Translated into several languages, the *Historia* may be the most widely-sold history of philosophy ever written in any language. For Marías, it gave the lie to the notion that the second Spanish Golden Age ended with the Civil War. His was the first successful publication by the brilliant post-Civil War generation of Spanish writers. Marías remarked that the success of the book may have been due to the fact that his insights came from first-hand readings, not from commentary borrowed from earlier philosophical manuals, a common—but rarely admitted—practice by authors of manuals of philosophy and literature.

Ortega had many brilliant disciples, among the most outstanding, José Gaos, María Zambrano, and Xavier Zubiri, and he impacted specialists in other professions: Laín Entralgo, Rof Carballo, Américo Castro, to mention only a few. But Marías stayed closest on task during the years Ortega spent exiled in France, Argentina, and Portugal, respectively. He extended and elucidated the Ortegan doctrine with such insight and depth that in his post-exilic years Ortega began referring to it as "our philosophy." For many reasons, among them illness, exile, and his philosophic style, Ortega left several loose ends in his work. He entrusted their completion to his younger collaborator, and Marías lived up to the task with his lifelong personal credo—*Por mí que no quede* (loosely translatable as "I do my part"). But in doing so, he did more. Now navigating the metaphorical Ortegan ship after Ortega's death, he sailed uncharted seas and mapped the new philosophical continent.

In comparison to Ortega's formative years, Marías' own circumstances were approximately reversed. Ortega found in the German universities of Marburg and Leipzig a dramatic sense of philosophy. There he discovered tradition and teachers—everything but a philosophy he could sink his teeth into and to which he could devote his life.

On the other hand, Marías found in Ortega—and to some degree in his other professors—a dynamic, promising doctrine that he adopted wholeheartedly but one he had to digest and appropriate on his own. His teachers convinced him, but at a deeper level he had to convince himself. He was steadfast in his loyalty to Ortega, but because of circumstances, his was a loyalty maintained at a distance and in complete independence from his mentor. These features were less than ideal, yet from another perspective not altogether negative. In fact, there were two advantages in their ten-year separation: first, it allowed Marías to see for himself not only the validity of the general Ortegan doctrine, but also glimmerings of its further possibilities which Ortega had not yet explored, or at least had not publicly mentioned. Second, it afforded him a margin of personal objectivity and introspective awareness about his relationship to Ortega and his philosophy. It is interesting to speculate what would have happened had Marías spent those formative years in close company with Ortega. Would the master's gravitational pull been too great, perhaps stunting Marías' own genius? And what would have been the effect on Ortega himself? It is interesting but idle to speculate further on these hypotheticals.

Unexpectedly, and doubly so for an intellectual out of official favor, in 1964 Marías was named to the Royal Spanish Academy, the highest Spanish honor and recognition for literary and intellectual excellence. Reportedly, the regime, now moving into its geriatric stage, was dismayed but grudgingly realized that it had no legal grounds on which to oppose the appointment and that to move against Marías would do it more harm than good. Its official silence, if not deafening was loud. (Not long thereafter, Spaniards began slyly resorting to a play on words to describe the Franco regime. Instead of *dictadura*, Spanish for dictatorship, they started calling it a *dictablanda* (*-blanda*, meaning bland). As for Marías himself, his growing prestige and following allowed him to speak and write with ever greater authority on many topics.

6. The Missing Dimension

As early as 1947 Marías had become aware that a whole dimension was missing from the Ortegan analytical or "intrinsic" theory of human life, cogently condensed in his *Cogito*—I am I and my circumstance. He made formal reference to the missing dimension in 1952 in an essay titled *La vida humana y su estructura empírica* (Human Life and its Empirical Structure). But though the idea was clear, the style was not. More than twenty years would pass before he attacked the problem.

Finally, in 1968 he was ready. During an intense, sixteen-month span he wrote his way into an unexplored dimension of human life in a book with the formidable title: *Antropología metafísica: La estructura empírica de la vida humana* (Metaphysical Anthropology: The Empirical Structure of Human Life [1970]. The wisdom of his long wait was evident. Not only does this book reveal an unexplored area of human life but a new way of writing about the human person. In effect, there is a noticeable acceleration in his thinking, marked stylistically by an increase in insights and *aperçus,* a greater boldness in drawing conclusions, and less reliance on what could be called "professional documentation." *Metaphysical Anthropology* is the capstone of his philosophy, and he always referred to it as his most important philosophic work. And once it was in place, instead of pausing to savor the achievement, his thought unfolded at a faster, surer pace. As he says in his *Memorias,* II (1989), "It is not by chance that since that moment, and despite factors of extreme gravity that would have seemed to prevent it, my intellectual output has been much greater than during any other time."

With *Metaphysical Anthropology* we enter yet another dimension of Ortegan philosophy, one implicit in the original doctrine but with which Ortega himself had very little to do. Yet once there we find ourselves not on an esoteric or abstract terrain but in that zone of life known to us by heart but obscured by its very familiarity. We could say, hidden in plain sight. But just as decades earlier Ortega had to revise the traditional philosophical lexicon and modify conventional genres to accommodate the "intrinsic theory" of radical reality, so in a similar way Marías was obliged many years later to create a vocabulary for his complementary "empirical theory." With this combination of theories Marías had the first comprehensive philosophy of physical life as we really live it, that is, "sexuate" life as a child, girl or boy, as an adult, man or woman, as an elder, man or woman, and all the transitional stages. Sexuate—translated from *sexuado*—is a word Marías created in Spanish to describe those attributes, which without being explicitly sexual, are socially distinguishing features customarily or historically associated with one gender or the other: dress, styles, cosmetics, behaviors, social expectations, prohibitions, activities, etc. Sexuate distinctions may include sexual activity in the life of most people, but not everyone; exceptions include infants, the elderly, and those celibate by profession or choice. Sexuate differentiations begin at birth—pink for girls, blue for boys—and continue throughout life.

This advanced philosophy deals with the oldest of human experiences. Until now whole segments of physical being have languished as presuppositions at the anecdotal level or were treated from biological, psychological, or anthropological perspectives. Now that these have become valid elements of philosophy, our responsibility is proportionately greater. We must retrace our steps to see how these empirical components enliven, justify, complement, and complete Ortega's intrinsic theory of human life as the radically comprehensive reality.

We remind ourselves that these maneuvers are really the classic philosophic method. The earliest meaning of *methodos* was "road" (*metá* + *hodos*, way), which suggest an image of one traveling back and forth along a road on constant alert. Heraclitus called it "the road up and the road down." Ortega's "Jericho method" is a variation of the same process. But to be more exact, we must say that rather than having a method, authentic philosophy is a method similar to what the sciences mean by the "scientific method," though necessarily more flexible and encompassing because of its complexity and wider scope. Nevertheless, responsible thought retains a recognizable profile regardless of the field to which it is applied.

This methodical dynamism is inherent in all authentic philosophy. Real human problems render it authentic, not the static problems inherited from former times, nor hypothetical problems invented out of thin air for demonstration purposes. In short, the real problems of philosophy are the problems of real people here and now and day to day. For this reason, the idea of perennial philosophy, *philosophia perennis*, which concentrates from age to age on an unchanging fund of problems, is a deeply rooted misunderstanding of what philosophy really is. In many regards the history of philosophy is consubstantial with philosophy itself, but not in all. When the identity is pushed too far and the dynamism of thought fades what we have left is not philosophy but a species of scholasticism. It resembles philosophy, as a corpse resembles a living person. The difference between them becomes clearer when we accept living philosophy as "responsible vision" (Marías' succinct description of authentic philosophy), which means that plenary understanding comes not from merely studying problems passively and academically, much less creating them as hypotheticals, as one might create a mathematical problem, but by entering into the to and fro dynamism of necessity and justification. Here we gain an important insight: in order to understand problems philosophically we must subject them to this internal movement, revisiting their origins and rethinking the successive stages of their development. As Marías does in his early book *Biography of Philosophy*. In this way we comprehend their biographical and historical trajectory, or in simpler language, their story.

In our circular "Jericho" movements around a problem we may be tempted by misleading alternatives, defective reasoning, and deceptive byways. There are always roads that would lead us away from our authentic objective. Hence, we must be alert and intelligent in order to stay on course and complete the conquest. The etymological root of intelligence is the Latin *eligere*, meaning to elect or select and, consequently, necessarily to reject, in short, to say "yes" or "no" and be able to give the reasons for our decision. It is closely akin etymologically to *elegance*, the graceful and timely way of accepting the appealing and shunning the sordid. (Ortega stood almost alone in his understanding of the philosophic significance of intellectual elegance, no doubt better than any thinker of his generation, and for that same reason his stylistic elegance, though widely admired was perhaps as broadly misunderstood.)

A brief but elegant narrative from Ortega's writings titled *Geometría sentimental* (Sentimental Geometry) will summarize several points of his doctrine and give us entry into Marías' empirical theory:

A man known to us only as A is in love with a woman named Soledad. The story offers few details, yet this sparsity will also serve our purposes as we proceed through succeeding levels of human life. We learn that Soledad has left the city for several days. In her absence everything for A has taken on a mournful, anemic coloring. Things still appear materially in their accustomed places, but for A his entire world, its nearest and farthest dimensions, has lost the radiance that her presence gave it. A understands now that the "geometry" of the city is not merely its physical dimensions but that without her enchanting presence is only a facsimile of complete reality. In her absence the city lacks a center; now it consists of mere peripheries. These continue to be present to his eyes but not to his interest. How different was his experience of reality when he expected Soledad to appear before him! Then, in contrast to abstract, impersonal spatial measurements, the longest road to her was the shortest distance. Now, the shortest distance is impossibly long if at the end she is not there to greet him. Other people rank high or low in his standing if they are her friends or strangers to her. Some are haloed with importance because they live on her street and may have spoken to her. Another person vacations in her favorite resort. A woman whom A passes in the street excites him momentarily because she wears a hat or a dress similar to hers. From behind, another woman resembles Soledad, and A's heart races in anticipation of meeting her. Then his spirit sags when he sees an unfamiliar face and learns the disappointing truth. All who touch her life are anointed beings. As Ortega puts it, Soledad seems to walk on a divine cloud shaped by A's emotional emanations. He realizes that Soledad is his center of gravity, his *pondus*, the stabilizing weight of his life that ordered and grounded all dimensions of his life. She overruled the cardinal points of the compass, for she alone was his personal reference point. As he walked the streets, his real location was a function of how near or far she was from him.

The short narrative ends as A realizes that the distant city where she is staying emerges from anonymity and takes on sentimental significance for him. As Ortega puts it, "It is a pillar of salt that becomes flesh again. Everything, finally, appears to alter its order and to become articulated in the meaning and under the influence of the new geometric center of sentimental attraction."

In our first range or level of understanding, which is an exercise in phenomenological perception, description, and analysis, we confine ourselves to what Marías calls the general "intrinsic" or "analytical" theory of human life which Ortega calls the "radical reality." It includes, among other features, circumstantiality, historicity, perspective, the "embeddedness" or "rootedness" of realities that appear in "my" life, the implication of sociality, and the elucidating narrative or living reason that shows the interconnectedness of events. Nothing in the short story of Soledad and A appears out of the ordinary. It is a familiar narrative of ordinary human life, yet fraught with significance hidden in its very familiarity.

Now we move to the next level of understanding, to a new Jericho perspective, that is, from the conditions that appear analytically as the necessary, defining components of general human life in its personal forms as they actually appear. Consider the most obvious features: Soledad is a woman and A is a man. Furthermore, they are in love, or at least A loves Soledad. Yet the analytical theory has nothing to say about love, nor does it dwell on the primary categories man and woman. Yet we know from experience that, generally speaking to be a man or woman is to be sexuately—and perhaps on occasion sexually—susceptible to the other sex in a series of relationships that may culminate in love.

The fact that A knows Soledad by voice and sight means that they have the aural and ocular senses of hearing and seeing. We also learn that Soledad has talked with privileged persons also known to A. From this we deduce—normally without thinking about it—that both she and A are able to vocalize, and in not in random sounds but in a specific, complex language that conveys sense, feeling, and many levels of symbolic significance. In their case the language is Spanish and they live in the Spanish culture. With this fact we take for granted many others: assumptions, enthusiasms, antipathies, events, prohibitions, beliefs, courtesies, interpretations, customs, and manners. We reasonably assume also that Soledad and A are acquainted with many other cultural features: foods, entertainments, fashions, public events, political and religious matters, laws, and an overarching code of conduct for each sex with their respective permissible ranges, boundaries, and infractions.

We are not surprised that Soledad wears a hat—though perhaps today we would be—and that she has a female anatomy: head, face, hands, limbs, and body. We consider it unworthy of comment and almost of notice that she dresses and adorns herself in certain feminine way that reflects her time, class, age, and personal tastes. Similarly, we assume that as a man, A has corresponding anatomical features and that he dresses in the style and behaves within the range of normalcies common to the men of his time and society. Without being told so, we suppose that Soledad and A are mature adults, though not elderly. For life experience has taught us that beyond or before maturity the consuming love that A has for Soledad is rare, if not grotesque. For example, we would consider erotic love to be monstrous between an elderly person and an infant. The fact that the permissible erotic range fluctuates from era to era in Western culture only serves to remind us of the temporal limits inherent in amorous relationships.

As we analyze their relationship further, we realize that we have a tacit "mortal" view of Soledad and A. We would concede as normal features of their biographies that they were born, grew up, and now find themselves at a certain relative distance on their personal path to death. We would mourn them if we learned of their death, yet we do not normally lament the fact that all persons, ourselves included, will one day die. The uncertainty of the hour of death spares us the anticipatory grief of its certainty. Surely one of the keenest tortures of capital punishment is knowing the precise hour of one's death. This mortal limit, set near or far from today, lends life an inherent dramatic tension and timeliness. Time is not featureless, cosmic time, but marked and punctuated by events. As normal persons, we sense that we have come part way on life's mortal road and have an unmeasured but finite distance still to go. This is why—one reason why—as the count of days grows and shrinks inversely on opposing personal ledgers, life grows more earnest and we are less inclined to kill time before it kills us. As the poet Marvell reminds his reticent lady, "Had we but world enough and time, this coyness, lady, were no crime."

None of these and other features—walking on two limbs, for instance—is described in Ortega's intrinsic theory. The general metaphysics of radical reality in Ortega—and for that matter, Heidegger's concept of *Dasein*—make little if any mention of sexuateness, sexuality, age, corporeality, emotions, or mortality. It does not consider language, styles, society, or actual circumstances and cultural mores. We could say that although these analytical theories fix a framework for the narrative and dramatic character of life, it is barely concerned with the personal content itself.

For the first time in philosophy, though not in common experience and fictional accounts, we move from human reality as a concept or premise to life in its concrete forms and everyday manifestations. In other words, we are ready to philosophize about the human person of flesh, bone, and blood. This overview gives us an overview of the "empirical theory" of human life. The next task is to flesh it out with specifics.

7. Worldly Installation and Mortal Finalities

To summarize what we have seen thus far, if at one level the story of Soledad and A is minimal, at another it is undergirded by an impressive number of tacit assumptions, only the most obvious ones are mentioned here. Yet without them neither their story nor any other human narrative would make sense to us. These unspoken assumptions constitute what Marias calls in another context the "communicability of circumstances" that permit not only our common dealings with people but also the imaginary transmigrations mentioned earlier. They allow us to enter into relationships with people we may never meet in the flesh, who, indeed, may be fictitious persons created or ideally begotten by artists and writers. Indeed, the fictional persons may far surpass their biological prototypes. Leonardi's *Mona Lisa*, for instance, is much better known than the obscure merchant's wife who may have served as her model.

Although the empirical theory of human life is philosophically new, the common experiences from which it arises are as old as humanity. Soledad and A are persons—fictional persons perhaps—in the common understanding of the term. Marías' innovation consists of acknowledging and organizing these unspoken phenomenological assumptions as Ortega described them and extracting their human significance. Using Cervantes as a historical example, Marías describes the empirical features of the writer's life and person—for instance that he was married and thus that he could have a certain relationship with a woman—and concludes with a categorical summary of the empirical theory of personhood: "To it belong all those determinations which, without being ingredients of the

[Ortegan] analytical theory, are not chance events, coincidental contents, or factual elements, in the life of Cervantes, but rather empirical yet structural elements previous to any concrete biography and which function as its *assumptions* that we can count on."

Personal life could occur in other forms and on other worlds—a common theme of science fiction—but the fact that it appears in this specific bodily form and in this particular world means that even though its characteristics are not prior and necessary requirements of the general or analytical theory, they are verifiable, empirical elements of all known human life in our world. They constitute, therefore, the area of our life subject to possible variability. Or to put it another way, they are the means, endowments, and instrumentalities by which human life actually occurs in this world.

This feature has important implications for the general theory as well. Even though we say that human life is circumstantial and necessarily so—I am I and my circumstance, as Ortega taught—we remain at an abstract remove from actual circumstances until and unless we deal with them here and now in our personal world and in our specific bodily being. If we lived on other worlds in other physical bodies, or even in this one with robotic enhancements, circumstances would still be an essential ingredient of our life, but different from those that describe our life here.

In this specific sense both the world and the embodied person I am are susceptible to modification. The world grows larger or smaller, complex or simple, menacing or compliant, in ways that have to do only secondarily with its physical dimensions. "Earth" and "world," synonyms of sorts, differ greatly in linguistic usage, as Heidegger hints in an insightful essay on art. "Earth" usually retains its physical meaning, but more often than not "world" is figurative and metaphorical, indicating a network of human and social relationships with many overtones, both positive and helpful or negative and harmful. Today we have made of everything a "world"—the political world, the financial world, the literary world, the sports world, and so on. (The unclear distinction in the Scriptures between "world" as the physical earth and the "world system" of man has caused some Christians to disdain the material world in general. The ambivalence is remarkable, and remarkably naïve, since these believers also consider the world, or earth, to be evidence of God's creative splendor.)

Our "worldliness" begins sensorially. We see, taste, smell, feel, and hear things in order to take a degree of possession of them for our need or gratification. But linguistically we proclaim a deeper ownership by naming things. For instance, regardless of whether one interprets the Garden of Eden literally or metaphorically—or both—the Hebrew writer expressed a deep truth when he describes how God instructed Adam to name the creatures in Eden. Nothing is fully ours until we can utter it. Our love becomes truly real when our beloved calls our name and charges it with love. A gifted poet once said that a man is not a man until he hears his name from the lips of a beautiful woman. And the Scriptures hint that we shall not truly know ourselves until God calls us by our real name that he alone knows and confers.

In modern times technology has extended our senses and our linguistic capability far beyond humanity's old limits. For example, we can communicate instantaneously with people thousands of miles distant. This is an example of how our empirically embodied life has changed dramatically almost before our eyes. These changes remind us that man is not a natural animal even though he has an essential relationship with the natural world. The same is true of history. As Marías observes, "There are no 'historical constants', only acquired historical determinations, though their duration may last throughout all of history from Adam to the Last Judgment." Naturally, these constants are usually much shorter.

Here we come upon a linguistic problem. Unlike English and most other Western languages, Spanish has what from an English language perspective appears to be two verbs of being: *ser* and *estar*. *Ser* derives from Latin *esse* and is related to "essential" and "essence." *Estar* comes from Latin *stare* and is distantly akin to English "stand" and to "stance" in "circum-*stance*" (literally an "encircling stance"). *Ser* indicates being somebody or something and has a sense of inherent or relative permanence, whereas *estar* is primarily a verb of location and movement, of circumstantially being somewhere and in some situation. But Spanish *estar* has a range of additional meanings much greater than its English cousin.

We can say, then, that *ser* indicates living or existing as such, while *estar* is the concept of being in a locative, situational sense, that is, being located in place and time. Ortega's celebrated *Cogito*—I am I and my circumstance—first posits essential being as *ser*. But his formula contains two I's, not two moments of the same I as Descartes states—I think, therefore I am—and the second I in the Ortegan *cogito* indicates that my being is not that of an isolated ego or detached "I," but is always circumstantial, locative being in the world, concretely in my world and in realities at hand here and now. Thus, being in the meaning of *ser*, which taken alone remains an ideal abstraction, is linked historically and temporally to the world by locative implications of *estar* in circum-*stance*. The following step, as we shall examine next, is Marías' empirical theory of where and how our being occurs in this particular world.

His references to our personal surrogates Cervantes, Soledad, and A reveal some of the general ways we are inserted in this world. Marías calls them "forms of installation." But so far we are still at the analytical level. The general analytic theory attributes worldly installation as such to human life, and Heidegger also spoke of *Dasein* as *In-der-Welt-sein*, being in the world. But not until we proceed to the actual modes of installation do we reach the empirical level that is unique to the Ortegan-Marisian philosophy. Marías states formally: "Installation is the empirical [actual] form of rootedness in human life as radical reality." As we analyze A's view of Soledad, we see that for him she is not merely in the world in a general way but installed in a series of specific "stances"—being as *estar*—and modes that for him make up Soledad's special, unique, and adorable features.

Other forms of installation include corporality, the senses, sexuate mores, language, age, class, caste, and race understood as a social and historical heritage. Installation must not be thought of as static states or conditions. They are also installations that presuppose movement. Life is not only what sometimes happens to me, but also, and more exactly, what is always happening to me and what I am always doing myself in order to continue living. As Marías puts it, "The forms of installation are, therefore, forms of happening: or if you prefer, forms for happening, inseparable from happening, without which they would lack meaning and reality."

Here he introduces the dynamic image of vectors of varying intensity. In mathematics a vector is a directed magnitude, which applied biographically may be understood in terms of centrality, marginality, attraction, repulsion, urgency, intention, indifference, and variable levels of significance. Seldom does a single vector drive the life of a normal person. Living is a matter of choice, which usually though not always implies a plurality of options and pressures. In vectorial terms normal life is a continual compromise and selection among the pathways we could choose to follow. Not that they are equally appealing. Their power and attractiveness vary. Some, like distant stars, exert little gravitational force on us, while others pull us mightily in their direction. When several act on us from different directions a compromise vector may prevail that does not coincide exactly with any of them. In summary, living is a competition and compromise between alternatives with varying coefficients of attraction and indifference.

The idea of vectors comes from mathematical mechanics, but the motor that drives them is intention, aspiration or desire. Life consists of desires and aspirations primarily because it is incomplete. The angular distance between where we are and where and how we desire to be appears as a vector, that is, an unreal but possible trajectory toward the fulfillment of a need or desire. From yet another perspective this desiderative vector gives a "slant" to things, meaning that we incline to them, or they to us. As Marías says metaphorically, "Things take a slant—always a dramatic one—when they are struck by the vectorial arrows of biographical projects."

This does not mean that this "slant" or "inclination"

necessarily indicates inherent virtue in the vectorial objectives. They assume a value and priority insofar as they are subject in some manner to the projects I pursue in order to enhance, complete, or save my life. My life, the life of anyone as far as we know, also has a "donative" quality that confers significance on objects and people according to my desiderative inclination and circumstance. For instance, a person may be variously a stranger, a friend, a lover, a spouse, an enemy, just as I may take a peculiar object before me to be a hammer, a weapon, an icon, a work of art, or an archeological artifact, and depending on my perspective and inclination, possibly all or several of these interpretations sequentially or at the same time.

I have mentioned "worldhood" without first provisionally disqualifying it as one of the vaguest terms in common language. But in Marías' lexicon it takes on a precise meaning. My world is circumstantial, which means, as we saw earlier, that it assumes a circular stance about me. But the relationship is not simply a passive location amid things. I incline proactively to things about me and they respond to me by assuming a certain slant, favorable or resistant, as a result. World is also earth, as we reminded ourselves earlier, and also Cosmos extending in all directions as the horizons, limits, and unmeasured ranges of my projective enterprise. Because of my centralizing position it assumes a circular, or from cosmic perspective, spherical, structure around me. We can say tentatively at least, that order, not chaos, prevails in my presence. Wherever I am, the world positions itself around me as its structural center.

Other forms of world installations are undoubtedly possible, other circumstantial paradigms could exist, but as far as our empirical scientific knowledge and experience go at this point, bodily human life occurs only within this earthly circumstance. Many people—scientists in particular—insist dogmatically that biological life must surely exist elsewhere in the cosmos, just as various religions make similar assertions from a spiritual standpoint. But passionate convictions about biological life in the Cosmos initially demonstrate nothing but their intensity. A few visits to the Moon have not altered the fact that man is still "earth-man," which means that we are empirically installed in this world and bodily formed from earthly elements. "Human" derives from Latin *humus* and the biblical progenitor of the human race is called *Adam*, Hebrew for "earth." Probably the Germanic "man" has a similar prehistoric etymological linkage to earth. The English term "world" is an interesting and possibly revealing combination of *Wer* and *eld* (Germanic for "man" and "age," respectively). The world is literally "the age of man," which suggests the possibility that different kinds of beings or persons will have, or have had, their respective "ages" on this planet.

In summary, I am at once of the earth and in the world. A major theme in Western thought and art is the heroic image of man pitted against the world and its monstrous forces, striving to assert his will against their immense inertia and weight. It is Atlas bearing the world on his shoulders, Hercules performing the twelve superhuman labors, or the Athenian philosophers debating methods of gaining intellectual mastery of reality. At the other human extreme there are, or at least have been, civilizations with remarkable technology but passive societies. Think of ancient Egypt or classical China, for example—in which resistance to, or subjugation of, the world in the dynamic, aggressive Western manner would have been unthinkable and probably unthinkably heretical. The gigantic proportions of Egyptian art and architecture were not a testimony to human grandeur but appear rather to have been a profound acknowledgment of superhuman powers under which Egyptians lived in nearly timeless submission.

But regardless of these variable social modalities throughout the human ages, in the first instance the world is neither a thing nor a combination of things but the *where* or *wherein* of my life. As such, it belongs to the general or analytical theory of life in the Ortegan or Heideggerian mode. Naturally, the world contains, and sustains, many things, but my being in the world appears to be of a very different manner of installation. Because I am a physical person, I am not merely intrinsically in the world at large but always personally and empirically somewhere specific. Everywhere I am is centrically "here," which gives eccentric meaning to "there" and "yonder." This means that distance is primarily a feature that I impute to things from my location. *Things are simply where they are; it is I who interpret them to be near or distant as a function of their circumstantial relationship to me. Distance is a human disposition imposed on reality.*

We are in the habit of analyzing—that is, examining reductively—the things that appear circumstantially to us. We do so in the assumption that things divided are things truer. For example, the various subatomic particles are surely scientifically valid, but we should remind ourselves at times that such components are the reduced entities of unreduced complex realities, and the complex is no less a reality than the simple. As we saw earlier, the abstractions of which much of modern thought consists are, by definition, things abstracted or subtracted from something more complex. Aristotle ponders the nature of happiness at length in his *Nicomachean Ethics*. Yet as far as I know, happiness itself is not substantive; it exists only as an abstraction. I have never seen, touched, or weighed it, and I dare say no one else has either. What we have experienced are happy moments and what we have seen are happy or unhappy persons. These are the realities from which happiness is abstracted and bandied about as things. Love, goodness, truth, life, and many other generic states are either abstracted from unreduced realities, usually and specifically from lovely, good, truthful, living persons or their ideal simulacra, or derived contrastively from the observation of behaviors in persons. I repeat for emphasis that one of the principal philosophic tasks must be to restore abstractions to the realities from which they were taken in order to understand them in their original, clarifying circumstances. If science takes the world apart in order to understand and utilize its components, philosophy reassembles it in order to understand how it functions and what it means in its unreduced wholeness. Both steps are necessary and, as far as we know, equally instructive.

If the most impressive triumph of the modern mankind has been its ability to manipulate material reality by analytically taking it apart and reassembling it in other configurations and put to other uses, its greatest failures arise from the assumption that human reality may be treated in the same way and with similar results. Thus, the analytical mind assumes that plankton and planets, Galaxies and governments, men and women, ought all to be reasonably expected to behave in the same scientifically lawful and predictable ways as we reduce them to their components. To take an obviously negative example, it is the underlying principle of the totalitarian ideologies that grew up as the alter egos of modern science. Only one thing goes wrong: the totalitarian paradigm eventually collapses in confrontation with the radically different reality of human life. In classic logic we know that an error in the premise swells to a greater falsehood in the conclusion. In time, perhaps an immensely long time, like water that wears away the hardest stone, human reality erodes the strongest ideology, asserts its own unique force, and gives mankind another chance at freedom and a new cycle of life. The problem begins by defining mankind with utopian materialistic precision and proceeding with the expectation that humans will behave accordingly. The rigidity of the ideological paradigm, which at first seems to be its strongest feature, turns out to be its fatal flaw. Life is like a plant growing in a rock cleft. The rock is strong but the plant grows inexorably, microscopically minute by minute and eventually the rock splits apart. To define is to exclude, delimit, and deny, and the more complex a reality is, human life especially, the more must be excluded, delimited, and denied in order to make it conform to the non-human concepts of precision, exactness, and invariability. Human reality is not precise but reasonable, not exact but exuberant, not invariable but dynamic.

This means that we experience another person's presence—if we look on them as persons and not as things—in ways that differ from my encounter with animals, and vastly more so with inanimate things. Material things appear to me phenomenologically, that is, as appearances, but as far as we can tell, we are not sensibly present to them in turn. We are aware of persons in ways that do not apply to material things, and being aware, are able to have personal relationships with them—friendships, antipathies, sympathies, collaborations, conversations, love, hate. On the other hand, as far as we can tell, inanimate realities form no impression and preserve no memory of us. They do not aggress against us with deliberated intentions, nor incline to us in a series of preferences, but either obey the natural patterns we call laws, or await impersonally the personal, desiderative agenda of our dreams to lend them significance. Things and we stand in mutual reference as the reciprocal sum of our possibilities, each needing the other in order to be what or who it is possible for us to be. Yet the interaction is not unilateral; while we may communicate with people, we can only commune in silence or in technical, imaginary, or artistic modes with natural things. They endure the exuberant overflow of our life as the objects of our projects, but since our life must be rich in experience in order to supplement their muteness and inertness with significance, the same impoverished solitude that youth normally detests may become the saturated solace of age. The judgments and sentiments these muted natural things elicit from us tell a story of our own life. Amateurs and tourists seek instant and easy aesthetic gratification in spectacular beauties and grand vistas. More perceptive persons generously lend these qualities, or others unseen, from their own fund of knowledge and love. The greater aesthetic test is not the easy appreciation of consecrated beauties and authenticated public vistas but humble scenes that never knew artist's coloring or poet's laud yet also pulsate modestly with cosmic meaning if we lovingly coax them into revealing themselves. Inanimate things are not alive, as we understand life, yet in our most generous moments and impulses, can we not sense in them, or perhaps lend them, a mute yearning for fulfillment, purpose, and realization, as quantum mechanics seems to be on the verge of discovering? The limited person complains that he cannot see the forest for the trees; the wiser among us see the trees but also glimpse their further significance and make of them a forest. The world appears as rich or rudimentary as we are.

The human meaning of things lies in the in-exhaustible possibilities they offer us. As Wordsworth says, "... the meanest flower that blows can give thoughts that do often lie too deep for tears." These nearly limitless possibilities correspond insofar as I can perceive and utilize them to my frontal, facial, and futuristic life. I am always installed somewhere, always doing something specific with my circumstantial world in a futuristic process called living. Exactly what, where, and how I am engaged is part of my personal narrative with its limitations of time, ambition, and ability. To put it more formally, the narrative of my life is the story of my actual installation in the world.

This installation occurs—with the inevitable exceptions that confirm the general dichotomy—in two general sexuate modes: men and women represented in Ortega's skeletal narrative by Soledad and A . . . By reconciling in *Metaphysical Anthropology* our common experience of "sexuate" and corporeal life with the Ortegan doctrine of life as radical reality and historical reason, Marías comes into full possession of another area of Ortegan philosophy. From this level, which he achieved in the fifty-sixth year of his life, he was to go on to write with impressive clarity, elegance and sympathy of the relationships between men and women. There is much to say on the topic. But let us be clear about where we stand and what we have covered so far. As Ortega might say, it is time to take another turn around Jericho.

Through Ortegan phenomenology we realize that everything we know, discover, or encounter, appears to us temporally, historically, and personally in "my" life. Formally speaking, we can say that all epistemology, the science of knowledge, is subsumed in the general science of human life, and to bring it to a personal point, in my life. But here we also find a momentous paradox, and as Marías tells us, a historical inflexion, or as I described it earlier, a tipping point, in the very concept of metaphysics, or theory of the real. Customarily, thinkers of nearly all sects and schools have treated the world and the things in which it consists as though they stood apart from our life, as though the more detached they were, the more rationally trustworthy and reliable our understanding of them became. Now we come to understand them from a different perspective: as realities that appear "rooted" in my life, the only mode of perceiving them.

Until now, Western metaphysics has devolved for ages on the idea of objects, including the ideal objects we call ideas, manipulated through the doctrines of idealism and realism, or from a personal perspective, as subjectivism and objectivism, that is, objects seen as volitional or desiderative realities and phenomena. To put it in simpler terms, objects appear as things existing apart from my life and mind as realities imminent and immanent within themselves: the elusive "thing in itself." We can identify this appositional or confrontational relationship hidden in the word "object". For etymologically, "objects" are those realities that are "thrown" or placed in our way (*ob*, before or against + *ject* (-*jectum* from *jacere*, to "hurl" or "throw").

But if we consider the entire phenomenological context, we see that objects alone cannot constitute a metaphysics; indeed, standing alone and in isolation could not be objects at all. Quite literally in order to be objects in the first place I must stand before them, as they must stand before me, in my way, resisting or facilitating my living. It is my life, the life I am shaping, that allows the objective and facilitative qualities of things to manifest as circumstantial reality. Taking a dialectical shortcut, we can say that objects are a component of my circumstance, not in the old realistic, physical mode but as a function of my dynamic drive to make my life. But to what I have just said, I must add that objects do not divide neatly into negative and positive elements. I need the resistance of objects either to temper and polish my life projects or abandon them for better ones. For if every human creation begins as a dream, as I claimed earlier, it becomes achievement only as a result of overcoming or utilizing the objective resistance offered by my circumstance. But by this same measure, we can say that the inherent possibilities of things, including the possibility of becoming objects at all, remain latent and unrealized without my dynamic ambitions, in short, without my life they are, or appear to be, listless and essentially meaningless. This means, further, that my final relationship with things is not primarily "objective," not reclusive and distant, but effusive, appositional, and intimate. Living requires that I reach out fearfully, confidently, or generously to things, and by doing so, I allow them to fulfill some of their objective potentialities. And their fulfillment is part of the dynamic process by which the world of potentialities becomes my world. Therefore, a truer phenomenological description of objects must include, or presuppose, the person for whom they function as objective possibilities in the first place. What I really find in my living quest is myself living with, among, and by means of things, always wary of their resistant qualities but necessarily avid for their facilitating help. Hence the dramatic tension—dynamic, felicitous, or tragic—of human life in the resistant world.

For ages these human relationships with things, people, objects were either taken for granted and dismissed as anecdotal details or later deliberately removed or reduced in the interest of so-called objective purity. In summary, the objectivity of things was regarded as absolute and impenetrable—things-in-themselves—instead of standing in circumstantial and metaphysically inseparable relationships to my life, the foundational or radical reality. *This was the tipping point, the inflexion of philosophy that Ortega discovered and Marías established as the human coordinates of a new philosophical method.*

My relationship with reality consists of a multi-dimensional, futuristic, and circumstantial configuration. The world is so astonishingly accommodating to my presence that, as we saw earlier, anywhere I am located becomes the circumstantial center of things *for me and them*. By living I organize the world. We could say that rather than standing in a detached, abstract, or eccentric relationship to reality, I am always central within it, even if I am eccentric to the world as others appear to experience it. Dwelling always at the futuristically inclined, circumstantial center, I am engaged in a dynamic series of acts and decisions we call living that must be narrated eventfully in order to be understood. And the first person needful of this understanding is myself.

From this narrative understanding we deduce another truth: if life may be understood at all, then it stands to reason that it is reasonable and that this understanding is communicable to other persons of similar reason. Life communicates with life. This is a fact, more, a truth, of incalculable significance that we shall explore later.

We alone are responsible for our life, though we are not alone.

Because living is a communicable enterprise, it is inherently social and responsive. Now a fact of singular importance emerges from this circumstantial cycle of reason, understanding, and correspondence: once I consider life in a truly phenomenological way, that is, without preconditions or inherited assumptions, *I find myself to be an embodiment of life in a very specific form. I am of course a person, but a certain kind of person we know as man, as another person nearby is acknowledged as woman.*

But despite the accuracy of what I have just written, it remains inadequate. For unlike our designation of inanimate things and biological beings by categories or species, we relate to persons by a name that identifies them personally and distinguishes them from all others. For this reason, every human relationship is potentially intimate. Any reference to a person without giving a name consigns that human to the category of "nameless," abstract people, that is, we acknowledge their presence but not their person and thus demote them to the level of things. By calling persons by a proper name, we elevate them above generic designations to a "proper" level separate and apart from "improper," unowned, generic realities. For this reason, it is an "impropriety" to attribute generic captions to individual humans, even though the limitations of language itself mean that for linguistic convenience we resort to such labels—mankind, humanity, society, men, women, and the like—when referring to large human pluralities. In several senses, however, including the religious dimension, personal life responds to a proper "name-calling," as God called out to Adam in the Garden of Eden.

For Marías perhaps the greatest error of modern thought has been its tendency to disregard general phenomenology in a rush to the general assumption that human life is derivative and, therefore, that it can be understood by reducing it to its presumptive antecedents—biology, chemistry, genetics, ancestry, and environment. The contextual truths of this general assumption make it all the harder to resist. For example, a child's physical body, those genetic factors that correspond to our old question *who?* obviously suggest parents and ancestors through physical resemblances. But not the child itself, not the *who?* that corresponds—and responds—to a proper name and a proper being that distinguishes it from all other persons, including close family members, even an identical twin.

This irreducibility of human life makes possible a whole range of relationships—love, friendship, intimacy—that otherwise would be inconceivable. We love or loathe a person not because he or she is just anyone, any-body, but because that person is unique, not any one but an only one who cannot be properly called by any name but the one proper to them: their own. With this we reach a momentous conclusion: the uniqueness of human life, the irreducible "who" of persons we vocatively acknowledge in our everyday relationships appears phenomenologically and experientially as *creation, a reality reducible to nothing previous or present*. As Marías puts it: ". . . creation becomes the only adequate manner of describing the origin of personal realities. The person as such is derived from the 'nothingness' of every other reality, for it cannot be reduced to any of them. If we do not regard it as 'created,' it becomes literally inexplicable to us, or appears as forcibly reduced to what it cannot be: a thing."

This irreducibility means that a person must be properly named, but the name does not constitute a delimiting definition. One's proper name points to life's internal propriety, intimacy, opacity, and potentiality. Human life is modest, at once revealing and concealing itself. The proper name we call another is our everyday acknowledgment of that person's uniqueness. In its superlative form this reticent internal life takes the form of intimacy, which in love and other relationships must be shared but cannot be exhausted. For life is not simply created and revealed once and for all but is always being created and revealed, and always subject to levels of concealment. Life is always a process of getting ready to live more and to personalize our world as we do so. All prior human life is the expectant prelude to greater vital becoming. This why it cannot be simply defined but can be understood in the fullest sense only as a narrative.

But I cannot live more without the world's circumstantial complicity in my surpassing effort. I need things and people in different ways in order to go on becoming myself. For if life is a creation, it is never a finished creation, at least not in its mortal duration. (We shall take up postmortem life in the Level III of this book, but it is important to acknowledge that it is also a component of our life here and now and cannot be dismissed without curtailing our story.) This means that my native intimacy must turn effusively to the world and reality of others if I am to intensify and extend my life toward a happier, fuller estate. My inner life, often mysterious even to me, but also projective and futuristic, has no alternative but the paradox of partially externalizing itself and its secrets to others and the world. Human life is, first and foremost, a matter of *expression*.

How do we express ourselves? Sonorously and vocatively in language, of course, but also in visual ways. Consider Marías' explanation: "... the secret intimacy in which that arcane person consists rises to the surface in the face—which is the person as he is projected forward." Here the word "face" also becomes verbal: we face the world in a forward and futuristic manner, we look ahead and express our anxieties and anticipations in our eyes, grimaces, and by words and body language. Therefore, we can say that our face is the physical correlate of the forwardness of life and the personal metaphor of our unfolding biography. This is why in order to know someone we must learn to read that person's face, particularly the eyes, the "mirror of the soul," the visual revelation of inner personhood. To cover the face, as some religious cultures do, appears to depersonalize the person, usually a woman, but upon further reflection we realize that it also enhances the arcane dimensions of that person. To conceal then becomes an incitement to reveal.

Just as the uncovered face itself reveals personhood, it may also conceal it. It seems deeply meaningful that the face, the personal feature that most readily identifies us, is also linked to *persona*, or *prosopon*, the theatrical masks worn by actors of Classical Greece and Rome who spoke their roles behind or through them. In this aspect our face is also our façade, concealing what lies behind it. This puts us on track of another aspect of personhood.

I repeat that both the people we meet and our own person are never in a state of completed being. The question looming before us is whether the process ends with physical death or continues beyond it. In this life they, and we, are always coming into being to the dissonance or resonance of former experiences, episodes, and aims. Personal reality is dynamic and dramatic, even though often life gives the illusion of being in stationary dullness. While there is life there are the changes of which living consists. If we chance to meet an old acquaintance after a long separation, it may take a moment to reestablish the relationship because of the changes in both of us that perhaps neither of us suspected. We are the same persons, yet not the same. We have both progressed in our life story, perhaps at different rates and in different directions. This is why childhood friendships often fade in mature life. As life progresses, our pathways may diverge, sometimes too much for easy reconciliation with our shared past. Life develops along the trajectories described by our vectorial intentions, which means that our biographies may no longer resonate, indeed may conflict. For the sake of old friendship, we may remain friendly though no longer friends.

Our life story appears primarily recorded on our facial features. We study another's countenance, and if we learn to read well—which is an acme of wisdom—we can decipher the quality of time lived and the personal history of triumph and failure. This requires seeing beyond the genetic or racial features of one's face and appreciating the person behind them. Abraham Lincoln once remarked that after about age forty we are responsible for our face. I take his comment to mean that sooner or later who we have become, or failed to become, is etched in our features. Our persona cannot forever conceal our person.

We assign time analogously to living creatures and inanimate objects. Everything living or lifeless has an age attributed to it. But is this attribution valid? It seems highly doubtful that it applies in the same way to inanimate objects. From our perspective, time is the ambiance, if not the substance, of eventualities that happen to us as we live, because we live, and in order to live. As Heidegger said, time is the horizon of every event included or implicated in _Dasein,_ which means, as I understand it, everything of which human living consists. Whether time exists in the same or similar way—if at all—for non-living realities is an open question that we shall defer to a later discussion of chronological and kairotic time and some of the questions it raises.

Therefore, human life is a reciprocal process that occurs "sexuately" as men and women. Men identify themselves as men only by reference to women, and the same is true of women with regard to men. Without the other sex it would be logically impossible to think of ourselves as a man or a woman—or an exception to both—just as we would not know the meaning of "north" if there were no "south" by which to define it appositionally. I say again that life is not a matter of precise mathematical boundaries. Its parameters are more general, generous and porous in their human inclusiveness.

Naturally, this radical sexuateness, which is the primary form of installation in life, is previous to sexuality and sexual preference as such. We are, or may be, sexually active for a portion of our life but we are sexuately installed from birth to death. It is much more than a purely biological matter. As Marias explains it, "This means that [the infant's] sexuate condition . . . is going to be interpreted socially. Since the child is not Adam or Eve but the inheritor of a tradition, composed of historical and social substance, so is its body, and of course its sexuality."

If it is true, therefore, that men and women are linked ontologically—that is, in their general installation as men and women—then the relationship transcends the modern flashpoints of legal and social equality of the sexes. Each gender functions as both the other's biographical reference and its possible fulfillment. And this means that a dynamic, shifting balance necessarily holds between them.

But if this is true in an ontological sense, that is, as a reciprocal relationship by which men and women define and know themselves as such, then why has history nearly always reflected a masculine point of view? If men and women share the earth in essential parity, then why has it always been taken to mean "a man's world"?

A preliminary explanation might be that history is much more than its official versions, which means that it does not have to be written to be real, as Unamuno argued with his concept of seamless "intrahistory." For Unamuno generations as such do not exist; what is real is the daily uninterrupted life of people. History as we commonly think of it is one thing, the whole human past is another, and a much greater other. Herodotus understood history to be a way of saving notable events from oblivion. But for everything preserved as chronicles of the past, much more is lost from human memory and probably by an immeasurable margin. Furthermore, even though "official" history relates preferentially the deeds and purposes of great or infamous men, forgotten or ignored history, the undocumented story of family life at home and marketplace, in the street and church or temple, would be more likely to acknowledge the equal importance to women.

But even if true, contemporary Western women are not satisfied with this condescending version of history. The fact remains, and painfully so for them and those who champion their cause, that this is, or has been, primary a world of male privilege, power, responsibility, and frequent abuse. It would require an irresponsible exercise in intellectual casuistry to deny that a condition of injustice has prevailed throughout history, in the

West certainly, and much more so in many non-Christianized cultures.

In this regard, it is interesting but understandable that these sentiments apply predominantly to Western women. Few in the West raise serious concerns about the status of women in Muslim, Oriental, or the inaptly named "Third World" societies in many of which by tradition and often by law the legal and social status of women is markedly inferior to that of their Western counterparts. Think of the disparities in divorce laws concerning property and parental authority over children. Yet this lack of concern for women outside the Western cultures is what we should expect precisely because Westerners have few expectations of cultures with which they share little common history. It takes an elevated degree of social commonality to create common expectations. These problems and demands are a part of the Western patrimony arising from shared core beliefs. We could say they are "family affairs," and despite what they may claim, Westerners have shown only modest interest in the way of life characteristic of other cultures, even those elevated enough to rival the West in one way or another.

In any case, neither the remedies nor the inequalities can be limited to Western women. The principle of sexuate reciprocity means that the injustice affects both sexes negatively, though, as we shall see, not in the same way. The evidence is all too apparent: in those societies where women have not enjoyed access to social discourse and professional opportunity, those that permit, and in some cases promote, what Westerners would see as the abuse of women, do we not see a general cultural degradation of men also? Where women are oppressed and ignorant, do we not also find a degraded society of oppressed and ignorant men? (This is why it can be problematic for a Western woman to marry a man from a comparatively repressive culture, especially should they choose to live in it. For within it pressures build on the husband to conform to cultural norms and subjugate the females in his family or suffer the consequences for nonconformity. As persons, they may truly love each other, but their respective cultures truly do not.) On the other hand, Alexis de Tocqueville saw in the comparatively elevated status of women in the young American Republic a major reason why the new nation had risen so fast and was poised to prosper much more.

Without gainsaying anything said so far, at the same time we need to be aware that many aspects of our contemporary society would probably seem unbearable to women—and men—of former times. What would a lady of the eighteenth or nineteenth century think of today's congestion, noise, crime, pollution, dangers, and haste? Would a woman of the Victorian era believe that the rough codes of social conduct and the vices of today's women represent an advance over her time and condition? Instead of envying our advantages, she might well pity us for our wrenching tensions and frenzied schedules, just as it might drive us to despair to have to live in her world. Apart from the demeaning features of all eras, we are all historically conditioned to live only in a particular society—usually our own—which means that comparisons of historical eras are necessarily biased and probably ought to be avoided if the intention is to demonstrate superiority or inferiority. Nor do the comparisons necessarily favor our age. Enlightenment historian Edward Gibbon considered the Roman Empire to be the pinnacle of civilization and blamed Christianity for its demise. But how many of us would prefer to live in the Roman Empire, a world without modern foods, plumbing, entertainments, transportation, medicines, and only rudimentary help for pain and disease? Today, average citizens have at their disposal technological wonders that not even the Caesars could dream of in Rome's Golden Age. We may rightfully admire the past and sing of its superior human virtues with late medieval poet Jorge Manrique. But if by some magic we were to experience it without the nostalgic coloring of time, no doubt we would quickly conclude that such a life is nightmarishly harsh and plead to be returned to our own time. The farther time separates us from events and people, the easier it is to replace them with our own ideal versions.

Marías declares that "In the whole history of the West woman has had to live in a world that has been fundamentally the world of man in which the majority of creations—at least the more visible ones having to do with 'things'—were masculine. Woman has had to live within this [masculine] world and shape for herself her own particular world within it."

Nevertheless, there were certain paradoxical advantages for women in this masculine setting. In eras that were especially restrictive the perceived eccentricities of feminine logic and reclusive behavior afforded her a margin of personal freedom, a limited but valuable vital space within which she could maneuver and pursue her own agenda without the excessive masculine scrutiny that controlled much of her life. It was a limited compensation for the legal rights she lacked. Modesty, coyness, reticence, demureness, and excessive clothing that bespoke a formidable moral perimeter were some of the ways woman kept her distance, and with it her mystery and mystique.

They added to her persona and to a degree shielded her person from the harsher features of male predominance.

Although contemporary feminists routinely interpret these acts and attitudes as proof of historical injustice toward women, they leave out another traditional advantage. Because she lived in a male-dominated world, women had to understand men and their ways, whereas it was not as urgent for men to understand women. Perhaps this explains why, as so many jokesters tell us with a strand of truth, women are able to manipulate men, even those—especially those—who may be, or at least think themselves to be, intellectually superior to women. She learned how men think and this allowed her to anticipate their actions and devise counter strategies, as the experienced hunter understands through keen and necessary observation the movements and reactions of prey and predator. As Marías declares, "... woman has had to imagine men, to place herself in his viewpoint, to perceive the structure of his reason, in order to lodge herself in his world and work out her own place in it." Whereas man proceeds in the name of rationality, or irrationality, its parasitical alter ego, and makes it nominally the foundation of his understanding of life and the world, for that same reason he often fails to understand the peculiar rhythm and unspoken premises of feminine reasoning. When Professor Higgins in *My Fair Lady* wonders why women will not think like men, he repeats what men have reasoned *illogically* for ages. Her circumstances explain the difference. How could she be expected to reason in the same way men do, if she must live so differently from them? Nothing could be more unreasonable than to expect her to do so.

But nothing in life is so permanent as change. In recent decades, as the cause of legal equality of the sexes advances in the West, we see that women are indeed beginning to think and act somewhat like men and, paradoxically, to understand them less. Their speech is coarser, their tone louder, and their clothing scantier. The repertoire of female vices now rivals the well-stocked male arsenal. Feminine modesty, demureness, verbal and bodily proprieties have faded noticeably in recent times. If the mere glimpse of a lady's naked ankle as she boarded a trolley was an erotic experience for a Western man of the nineteenth century, now the sight of a woman's body clad in the briefest of briefs causes no particular social commotion.

But this apparent sexuate convergence of the sexes is not exactly what it seems. Women adopt vices once considered male prerogatives as one way to rebel against a history of restrictive femininity and corresponding male predominance. For women what once were old vices now serve a new cause, whereas for men they are simply a traditional custom taken to new extremes.

As we saw earlier, because human life is an intimate and often arcane reality, we must express ourselves in order to engage the social world. Yet this involves a paradox: normally we reveal ourselves with words, facial expressions, and hand gestures. Generally, the human face and hands are uncovered in the Western cultures, the body only occasionally. But this bodily concealment may also be an inverse form of personal expression. The clothed and concealed human body is also a visible if silent component of our narrative. In confirmation or contradiction of our verbal accounts, our body mutely speaks a language of its own and has its own mechanisms for lying and telling the truth.

The face is the most personal human feature. We cannot say, for instance, that a man is handsome or a woman beautiful without referring primarily to their face. The human body without a face is disturbingly impersonal, a mere torso lacking personality.

What do we see when we look at a human face? Earlier we commented generically on the face. Now we extend those comments to include sexuate differences. Then we described life as indigent, mortal, and incomplete. But in his relationship to woman, man aims for strength, knowledge, and certainty. As Marías writes: "Man is ignorant; he does not know what to cling to, he is weak, he is threatened, subject to constant insecurity, destined to failure, condemned to death. And yet, man's aim . . . consists of the exact opposite: knowledge, strength, power, security." Does this mean that man is a mere fraud, pretending to be what he is not, as some modern theorists describe him? It is important to distinguish between claiming strength, knowledge, and power and striving for these qualities. The honest man knows that he does not possess all the strength, knowledge, and power he seeks. Otherwise he would not have to seek them in the first place. He strives for these traits even though he does not fully possess them because these qualities define what it means to be a man. Manhood consists of standing for strength and knowledge without necessarily possessing them. Naturally, like all things human, this manly aspiration can be avoided or denied. Man may reject the disjunctive polarity with woman that requires him to be strong, secure, and knowledgeable. He may try to evade manhood by overindulging in games, drinking, or partying. Often these surrogate activities lead to prolonged premanhood adolescence (the noticeable phenomenon in recent decades of the overage teenager who grows older without growing up.).

Marías agrees with Aristotle that these manly qualities can be summarized as *valor*. It may be understood in the traditional way as bravery in the face of danger, but even more so in a modern context as steadfastness amid daily challenges and moral mediocrity. In this context, valor reverts to its etymological meaning of "value" or "worth." For the brave man is valuable or worthy, as Aristotle noted.

All these qualities, or their lack, mark a man, and primarily in his face. I repeat that the human face is the visible metaphor, the summary narrative, of life's frontal, futuristic voyage. We live in a forward manner and metaphorically the face is the prow of life. This is why a faceless, directionless human torso mentioned earlier is so disturbing. Without a face, we cannot read the personal narrative and instead of human understanding, we are limited to impersonal physicality.

How then shall we describe a man's face? First, it registers the seriousness of life. Beyond his handsomeness or ugliness, his joviality or sadness, his racial or ethnic features, a man's face reveals the responsibility of life, which we may summarize as *gravitas*. In it we see how he has come to grips with the duties assumed or thrust on him. Or, alternately, how he has shirked his destiny; we read his failures and false resolve in his face, or we detect his courage, valor, and virtue. (The latter term, though historically especially associated with women, derives from *vir*, a Latin word for man, which is closely akin to old Germanic *wer* with the same meaning.) A man may hide his motives, nobility or frivolity for a time, but not forever; eventually his facial record reveals who he really is.

In contemplating the feminine face we begin with an expectation of beauty. But does this mean that we must exclude many women, perhaps the majority? For not all women are beautiful, just as many men, maybe a majority, are not strong. But just as man strives for strength in order to be a man, so woman traditionally has tried to be beautiful in order to be a woman. This is why, to hear Marías tell it, "The woman who does not try to be beautiful does not function as a woman; she has withdrawn from her condition." In our era many men avoid manhood by extending adolescence, or at least trying to extend it, and likewise many women prefer girlhood to womanhood and prolong it far past the limits set by previous generations. In the Romantic Age women were considered mature, even matronly, by the age of thirty. To no one's astonishment today, women at thirty or well beyond still refer to themselves as "girls."

However, it is not enough for a woman to be beautiful by objective, external standards, not even in the eyes of men. A woman, whether objectively beautiful or not, must believe that she is at her best in order to be her best. This is why wise women dress and groom themselves less to please men than to satisfy themselves. Most of us have known women, beautiful to us and others, who are ugly in their own eyes and reject all arguments to the contrary. In terms of a woman's self-esteem, beauty is not primarily in the eyes of the beholder but in her own mind. Women are at their peak when they feel themselves beautiful, just as man thinks himself manly when he is secure and comfortable in his manliness.

Of course, beauty is not an exclusive property of women. Men may also be harmoniously beautiful in form, voice, movement, and manners. But theirs is a different sort of beauty and many languages have different words to express it. In English, for instance, women are "beautiful" or if young, "pretty," but men are "handsome," or "good looking." Feminine beauty in a man is usually disturbing and we scarcely know what to make of it. To say that a man is "pretty" or "dainty" would suggest unimpressive manhood and perhaps effeminacy. A woman may say with varying degrees of admiration that a man is "cute," but for a man to apply the term or the equivalent to another man would likely be considered disrespectful and derogatory.

If masculine handsomeness is a pleasing addition, feminine beauty is primary; it is the first feature we hope to see when we look at a woman's face. Perhaps this is why harshness in a woman's looks, speech, and demeanor is—or was until very recent times—normally unpleasant to men. Yet the same quality may be admirable in men under certain circumstances, for example, in a military commander.

Naturally, cultural norms nuance the concept of beauty. For example, some cultures consider, or have considered, plump or even obese women to be especially attractive. In others plumpness is repellent. But it would lead us too far afield from our purpose to comment further on such cultural variables.

Even if a woman is not physically beautiful, her features suggest it. Her face is less massive and more graceful than the masculine facial profile. At first meeting, men experience a fleeting disappointment if they do not discover beauty in her features. Yet their predisposition to feminine beauty earns her a certain preliminary credit simply because she is a woman. Novelist Dostoevsky wrote that a woman is half beautiful merely by being a woman. Women symbolize beauty even though they may not personally possess it themselves.

In the presence of an exceptionally graceful or beautiful woman man often feels—and older generations used to say so—that she is too good for him, or any man, for that matter. Add to this the higher moral standards that traditionally characterized woman, and she seems too fine and beautiful a creature to enter into intimate union with his coarser, heavier features and perhaps less than exemplary moral record of his life. (Biblically, she was created at a remove from Adam's coarser clay.) Man sees her willingness to accept him, more, her enthusiasm for him, as a gift he does not merit, a treasure he cannot earn. Thus, in courtship, dressed in his finest attire, trimmed and groomed to soften his rough features, and in the best setting he can offer her, he traditionally proposed to beautiful woman on bended knee as a sign of the gratitude he felt for his unmerited fortune. Antiquated stuff, we may scoff today, yet tradition preserves kernels of historical truth.

Thus, the match is made. As the sarcastic saying goes, "He pursued her until she caught him." But there is truth in it. For he longs to possess her bodily gracefulness and facial allure. Her beauty or its enticing surrogates enchant and provoke him, lift him out of his heavy manly condition, lighten his life, brighten his attitude, quicken his steps, and stir in him loftier resolutions than he has ever felt before. Hear Marías' description: "Woman is stimulating because her function is to set man in motion, to call him; this is why she can be pro-vocative, a word that would be inapplicable to the masculine kind of attractiveness."

This enchanting woman may provoke a trace of ontological panic in the enamored man. Her charms and beauty are the magic that promise to rapture him out of his ponderous condition, his heavy male *gravitas*. But she may also elude him unless he acts quickly to claim her. In classical mythology woman is the nymph that entices man with delightful beauty but dances nimbly just out of his grasp and may vanish at any second. This is why in man, love and desperation, joy and anxiety are alchemically never far apart.

But the gambol of life and love is not yet in full play. If woman eludes man at first, her elusiveness is also an invitation for him to pursue her—if he is interested and she finds him interesting. If he woos and pursues her, becomes her "suitor"—its Latin root indicates one who follows or pursues—then his anxiety delights her. For she knows then that he is worth her time and attention. She is never so elusive that he cannot overtake her if he really wishes to and if she lets him catch her. For that reason, she reserves her keenest indignation not for the awkward but devoted suitor, not even those not to her liking, but for the half-hearted man who lets her get away.

But if he presses on and she says yes to his proposal, then woman shows another side of her feminine condition. Her elusiveness ceases, she runs no more, but stops, stays, and prepares to put down roots. No longer the elusive nymph, she now becomes the nester, the homemaker, though still cautious of his intent lest he take her for granted.

For now she faces a disturbing doubt, and it may show at unguarded moments in her face. For man, who lives solidly planted in the world, who feels responsible for it and who, like Atlas, bears its weight on his shoulders, also has another side to his life. At the same time an ontological wanderlust tempts him. Distant horizons beckon and far frontiers lure him. He thinks of other lives he could live and other worlds he could explore. Even worse, once aroused to love, man may be tempted to become a romantic butterfly, flitting from flower to flower. Woman's abiding fear is that once man is provoked into motion he may not stop when she does, that her charms cannot domesticate man's adventurous spirit. No doubt this is also one reason why she is wary of his high ambitions and senses in them a threat to the home, family, and security she now covets, that is, if she is now a woman and not simply still a playful nymph.

The so-called "war of the sexes" is more theatrical than real. Normally the sexes are enthusiastically attracted to each other because of their reciprocal relationships. The general rule of life is that men and women incline to one another in order to realize the greater possibilities of their life. This dynamic equation is taken for granted and thus goes largely unnoticed, while today the exceptions and failures draw most of the attention. Indeed, instead of confirming the general rule, the exceptions press for normalcy and acceptance.

At the other extreme, we find that Freudianism and its psychological relatives and descendants in the arts and social sciences rest on the assumption that what we have referred to here as "sexuate" relationships, including intersexuate friendships and family bonds, all turn out to be upon analysis thinly veneered sexual attraction. For Freudian-based psychology every family is a nest of subliminal incest. But this amounts to an animalistic reduction and simplification of the human person. We can only speculate about the advances in human understanding Freud and his followers might have made had they been able and willing to distinguish between the "sexuate" and the "sexual," a distinction that is foundational in human life and society but only hinted until Marías identified it and gave us the proper terminology to deal with it.

An error of even greater magnitude, so argues Marías, is to confine the balance of the sexes to legal and political equality while ignoring the living human reality that consists not of a static equilibrium but of a shifting, dynamic balance between them. As desirable as it is for legal, ethical, and religious reasons, sexuate equality cannot be simply a matter of women "catching up" to men, as though the latter were stationary, but of altering the dynamism affecting both sexes. If their relationship can be compared to a waltz, then each step of one partner is matched and compensated by a counter step by the other in order to maintain the sexuate rhythm and harmony.

This brings us to the pinnacle of empirical experience in the amorous condition. Marías agrees with a good many modern-day thinkers, psychologists, and pastors by telling us that love cannot be reduced to feelings, sexual acts, psychic states, or psychological predispositions, not even our enthusiasm for persons of the other sex. But he goes further by explaining love from our structurally reciprocal sexuate need that "happens" or "befalls" dramatically, vectorially, and plot-like in our life narrative. This description is packed with significance. Let us proceed in stages to clarify its meanings.

Customarily we busy ourselves with persons and impersonal things outside ourselves. As we saw earlier, a principal experience consists of expressing our inner life. We have no choice but to reach out to the world, to show ourselves in varying degrees. The outside world presses us always, urgent, demanding, threatening, promising, at once perilous and provocative. And the most provocative of all is love. Consequently, we do not at first know what to make of it. Psychologist Theodor Reik argued that our first impulse may be to resist it. Love demands the ultimate in risky but necessary self-expression. This is why what lovers do most is talk to each other, even though Hollywood would have us believe that love is a matter of bedroom acrobatics and audience voyeurism. When real love comes over us, suddenly we are illuminated and transformed by an experience that seems to be an eruption at the core of our being yet at the same time far beyond it. Our astonishment appears embedded in the curious way we describe it in English, to *fall* in love, which suggests that it happens unexpectedly by "chance" or "accident." Both are Latinate words built on the root verb *cadere*, "to fall," which suggests things unplanned, unexpected, and with a hint of chaos.

But if this lovely "fall" may happen unexpectedly at any specific time, it is not accidental over the course of a normal life. Instead we are predisposed to love, or to put it more formally, human life reveals a fundamentally "lovely" or "amorous" predisposition. Nevertheless, this does not mean that our inclination to love will necessarily culminate in love itself, just as the pursuit of happiness does not guarantee that we shall ever overtake it.

Once we fall in love with a person, our love story becomes our life story. But it does not begin the day we meet that person. Instead, it flows back retrospectively to include our previous life and the beloved's past. We want to know everything about the person we love and now we see that everything in both lives was a preparation for this love. We are persuaded that our entire life is now subsumed, justified, and contained in our love. We know now that love is not a thing, episode, or act, not something we do with a lover—although because of it we may do many things with the beloved—and thus is not a completion at all. Instead, it is state of being that consists in always coming to be, of becoming. We may use much of the same language that applies to life and living, for loving is living, only at a superlative level and with greater intensity. Once we are in love, we see our former life as preparatory and preliminary. Suddenly we realize how impoverished our life was before love revealed undreamed of possibilities.

On the other hand, if I need food or water, I can point to my biological or physiological need for these things. But in order to explain why I have an amorous need of a person, I must tell my intimate biography. This is why the genuine language of love is always to one degree or another, a mutual confession. Real love is the arena of the greatest personal truths, just as its counterfeits spawn the greatest personal lies. From this it follows that we may rightly have our doubts about a lover reluctant to talk of love. Love gives wings to the flightless and words to the mute.

It may be that I also have a limited need of persons for other reasons: physical strength, knowledge, manual expertise, companionship, protection, etc. The need is still real and it may lead to personal relationships such as friendship. But unless it includes mutual acceptance and appreciation, it veers toward the impersonal, with the possibility of dehumanizing the relationship altogether as in the case of loveless sexual relations. By definition and the confirmation of experience, dehumanized relationships lead not to personal enrichment, but to a coarsening of personhood. Without love, we come to loathe what seduces us, which when prolonged addictively becomes a degenerative decline into self-loathing.

Alone, I am a contingent creation, as philosophers used to say. The Ortegan Cogito "I am I and my circumstance" is not a declaration of monadic, self-sufficiency but a formula for its possible fulfillment. Amorous love of another person is archly personal. We could say to the second power, because it is really two conjoined stories. It arises from my biographical incompletion, what we can call my ontological indigence, the initial poverty of being. This means that my amorous need of the beloved person is the way to fulfill my life by becoming the person I was born to be. For above all else, happiness is becoming the person we were meant to be. And we do so by allowing and helping the person we love to become who they were meant to be. Here begins the intense dual richness of the truly amorous relationship. Could we not say as a result that "we are we and our conjoined circumstances, and if we do not save them then we shall not save ourselves"? For the person I love is also always coming to be. Love exists in a dynamic duality in which two unitary life installations co-implicate each other in a biographical, vectorial fashion. Our amorous need of another person is not a given, but a giving. Of what? Of myself, and not once only but in principle for all time to come. More than a gift, or an exchange of gifts, it is a mutual giving that keeps on giving perhaps forever. Love is mutual altruism and sacrifice whose main risks and temptations are selfishness and egotism.

The first thing lovers promise each other is that their love will last forever. To any true lover finite love, love promised only for a season, seems an amorous blasphemy. In the midst of finite mortality, love promises eternity. Perhaps we smile skeptically at lovers' promises. Do they forget in their euphoria that death intervenes to cut short their idyll and that life itself can be fickle and inconstant? Yet we lack the logic to contradict their seemingly contradictory vows. Love overmatches skepticism.

But here at least we can pause to rethink some things in a cooler frame of mind. Love is a story, but also an open book that cannot hide its contents. It is said that love cannot be hidden. Yet experience tells us that if nothing promises more than love nothing breaks its promises more often. Does its capricious record call into question all that we have said about the amorous condition of human life? Not at all, only its counterfeits.

While we are at it, we may as well admit other unhappy aspects of the human love story. It comes to us laureled with myth and haloed by magic, but also trailing a sordid history of deceit and heartbreak. The fond theories of classical philosophers and psychologists treat it in a torrent of analyses, studies, and popular articles. (Though curiously today its substitutes and surrogates are more popular.) If love stands, or once stood, as the pinnacle of earthly ideals, it is also the most democratic of calamities. It spares neither simpleton nor genius. The Greek thinkers viewed erotic love as the supreme human tragedy. Were they right? We find ourselves conflicted and cannot give an unequivocal answer. But in any case, its failures do not abash us for long. Every generation discovers it anew. For lovers it is ever newly born, full of bright promise and bearing no responsibility for its mistreatment of past generations. Every love is a first love. Every love is an only love.

A generation ago youngsters came up with the catchy phrase: make love, not war. Now in middle age or beyond, they do not weary of repeating that love is the panacea for the world's ills. In an ideal sense, no doubt they are right, but prudence cautions that love is a risky venture. We get into trouble much sooner over whom we love than whom we hate. You can hate whom you will and nobody takes any particular notice. But announce your love of the wrong person and storm clouds immediately darken your horizon.

At about that same time the cliché of "free love" became

popular along with the defiant reminder that it was nobody's business but the lovers'. But wiser people always knew better. Love is personal and private in one dimension of life, but everybody's business in another. For society must live with the consequences, good or bad. Those who abuse their health make similar claims, but society as a whole pays eventually for their folly. More importantly, life is born of love, which is why despite current arguments to the contrary, love continues under considerable moral and legal restraints, or flouted, considerable pain.

But let us be clear about the kind of love are we talking about. For though we acknowledge several species of love—*agape*, *filia*, *eros* in Greek, for instance—the English language must make do with a single overworked term to designate them categorially. In addition to erotic love, we generally acknowledge other forms of love or devotion: parental, filial, and sibling affections, intrasexuate and intersexuate friendships, patriotism, love of mankind, religious fellowship, and for some, the love of truth. (Upon reflection I suggest adding religious faith to the list. We call it a belief, but it seems to be a unique kind of love. I shall explain my reasons in the third level of this writing.)

For Marías, heterosexuate love is not merely a species of the genus or genre called 'love'; instead he thinks the contrary is true: "I do not believe that this love [heterosexuate love] is a species of that genre but rather that all the other forms of love spring from intersexuate love as the basic form of personal need." He states in another writing: "This love between man and woman is the concrete nucleus of the very broad amorous condition. By this I mean that the latter orders itself entirely about the former. This is not to say that all the 'loves', in the broadest use of the term, are modifications or transformations of this heterosexuate love but rather that love is rooted in that [amorous] structure which is precisely heterosexuate."

Here the Pauline description of divine love also correctly summarizes our amorous relationship with a person. We live, move, and have our being in love. But we must point out that unlike religious love, or love of mankind, heterosexuate love is preeminently exclusive. It exists only for one special person and renders the true lover essentially indifferent to all others. Sexual attraction often passes for sexuate love, but its promiscuous inclination reveals the gulf that separates them. Essentially bodies are sexually interchangeable, but no one else can replace the unique facial presence of the beloved person, not even a physical twin. This is why those who pay more attention to the body than the face of the beloved are not really in love. Saint John of the Cross explains that love settles for nothing less than the physical, facial presence of the beloved:

> The pangs of love nothing can efface
> Save the beloved's figure and face.

Thus we live life in "lovely" susceptibility. Every initial sexuate encounter is slightly charged with this inchoate possibility. Unlike our contact with things, sexuate encounters exhibit the normally evanescent but pleasing possibility of ontological happiness. Desired objects may also offer passing pleasure and hints of happiness. But these hints are seldom permanent.

But if such an encounter prospers and we fall in love, the lover who embodies it meets, or appears to meet, our expectations of happiness. But this happens only by giving oneself to the beloved. From this it follows that henceforth the lover who offers us this happy fulfillment becomes essential. We claim happiness as ours, but paradoxically it resides in another person. For this reason, even the unhappiest of lovers, thinks that his love is worth all possible heartaches and would not trade it for the tranquility he knew before he fell in love. Romantic poet Campoamor romantically exaggerates the pangs of love, but tells a truth in doing so:

> Everything in love is sad, but sad and all,
> it is the best thing there is.

The lover has no real choice to but say yes to his love, even a tragic love, because anything else would be to say no to himself. One may die for love, but to deny love is worse, for it is a denial of life. To fall in love is to experience a transformation of the human condition similar to a religious conversion, which is a kindred kind of falling in love. In both kinds of love old things pass away, all things become new. Yet in all but the most reckless souls there is a brief hesitation, perhaps even a resistance, as we saw earlier, before assenting to love's lovely fall. We know that we are staking our life on the move and we may lose the gamble. Love takes us out of our safety zone, and there love may fail in its promise of fulfillment and become what Marías calls "irrevocable painfulness."

Thus, our deepest calling, our primal vocation, is not egotistical concern for self but altruistic devotion to another person. If our devotion is to a human person we call it amorous love, if to a divine person we know it as religious love, for the two forms are close kin, though by no means identical. Our first purpose and supreme hope in this world is to become the person we were called to be, and love in this dual sense is the highest form of that calling. By transforming us, love phenomenologically alters our world. In love we find meaning where before we found only monotony, sense where we saw only nonsense. Beauty now glows around the most pedestrian realities; for ugliness has surrendered its control over creation. We commune with sectors of the world that before knew only our indifference. Beauty claims a renewed priority in our affairs, and radical harmonies filter through the once drab fabric of creation.

The cynic would say that all this has happened countless times in other lives. No doubt it is statistically true. But never before did it happen to us, never personally. All real lovers know that their love will never be duplicated, and in this irreplaceability there is a hint, perhaps a proof, of the incomparable worth and uniqueness of their life. And if their spirits are generous, of all personal life.

The rapt attention lovers pay each other is not a matter of obsessive or possessive curiosity. In discovering the intimacy of the beloved, lovers also catch a glimpse of themselves in the other's eyes. Perhaps this helps explain the odd sensation of recognition lovers experience in their facial and verbal encounter with the beloved. In love and in faith we discover ourselves as we discover our beloved.

Here a distressing question implied earlier must now be asked directly: if love is our most authentic calling, why does it often end ingloriously? Marías suggests that one reason may be insufficient imagination. Taking his cue from fiction, which often intensifies life, he points out that although Don Juan, the world's most notorious lover, for instance, could provoke love in many women, he could not project it beyond physical eroticism. Love is biographical, which means that it must projected, imagined, and its plot expanded and intensified over time. Don Juan knew only amorous beginnings. Hence his paradoxical failure as a lover. For ideally love calls for a lifetime of exploring the inexhaustible mystery of the beloved person, what Marías calls "the progressive discovery" of the beloved, bearing in mind as we saw, that the discovery is a dual discovery. It calls for a level of generosity and dedication that goes against the grain in our era, or any era for that matter. The emphasis on self-aggrandizement and the visual, impersonal glamor of the entertainment industry invites our admiration but does not return it, demands our devotion but rarely reciprocates. It is a poor school for lovers.

If human life culminates in love, then it stands to reason that to weaken the case for love is to weaken the case for life. This is why love does not favor those who live on borrowed dreams and anemic enthusiasms. Love reveals to the soul-weary that they are better people than they knew and lifts timid imagination to higher domains of beauty and happiness. But love's nobility will not suffer adulterations but soon abandons those who would mistake it for entertainment or a cure for boredom.

Love, which above all else offers the happy plentitude of life in this world, by that same measure urges us to anticipate the fullness of life in the next. It is probably not by chance that the noticeable decline of lasting love in our time matches the growing indifference to personal immortality. And one reason seems obvious: if we continue being ourselves in the next life, a loveless finite life in this world hardly kindles an enthusiasm for infinite life in the next. Instead of happiness, immortality seen in this light might turn out to be everlasting hellish loneliness.

Described in this sense, hell would be the domain of the loveless and the intensification of everything wrong in this life.

For uncounted ages mortal life offered little to common people. From our contemporary point of view, theirs was a short, brutal life of drudgery, illness, ignorance, and poverty. What we call the "third world" today probably resembles what was the only world for the majority of mankind in former times. Because the people of earlier times had so little to look forward to in this life, they had all the more to hope for in the next. But the truth be told, today in the "first world" few are eager to leave this world, which for millions of persons is replete with food, drink, entertainment, travel, conveniences, necessities, and luxuries. By honest comparison to what we are accustomed to in this life, the traditional description of the Hereafter sounds dull and unappealing. For this reason, we shall add the theme to the mounting number to be considered in the third level of this book.

With this we come to an enduring paradox of human life. Our only hope of life fulfillment lies in the future, but there death awaits us, appearing as the annihilation of that hope. We live our life in pursuit of happiness, but our pursuit must one day end. Despite our best efforts, we must leave many things undone, in some lives with resignation, in others in hope of more life to complete them, in still others, relief that we are shed of the burden. We accumulate years but only after they are void and spent, and if nothing else we see without excuse or subterfuge that as we saw before, we are *mortals* who are also *moriturus*, mortals who must die. This is the empirical fate of mankind; human life is a closed mortal structure, a story with a beginning, a development, and an end. Is there more? We shall present the case for it in Part III.

In the last decade of the twentieth century Marías refined and summarized the quintessence of his philosophy in *Razón de la Filosofía* (The Reason of Philosophy [1993]), *Mapa del mundo personal* (Map of the Personal World [1993]), and (*Persona* [1995]). These titles were by no means his total production. He continued to write on many topics, including the cinema, to which he was especially drawn all his life.

Don Julián's health failed in the spring of 2000. A debilitating heart attack cut short his activities and obliged him to depend on friends and family for his basic needs. But even though his strength and stamina were spent, his photographic memory and positive spirit were not. He suffered unbearably for five years, yet never complained about the pain. He dictated articles when he could no longer type them and spent months, so he confided, reviewing in his mind and by heart everything he had ever written and quoting from memory his favorite poets in several languages. He would have done more had a longer earthly life been granted him. For as it turned out his personal credo was not quite accurate: by the standards of ordinary mortals he did far more than his share. But his time had come, that is to say, it had gone. He was satisfied with the life he had lived. As a child he had vowed never to lie. None ever crossed his lips and no grudge followed him to the grave. His faith was intact, his fidelity to truth unbroken, his enthusiasm for life undiminished. His religious faith never wavered, and he had no doubts about immortality but spoke hopefully of continuing in the next world what he had begun in this one. Near the end he said that in this life we do what we can with the possibilities at our disposal. But inevitably the mortal moment comes when we must leave our plans and projects in the hands of God to do with them as he sees fit.

There is no way to describe all that Marías accomplished in his seven decades of intense intellectual work. He was a person blessed with extraordinary talents and therefore charged with uncommon responsibilities. He lived by the principle inherent in his faith and his philosophy that to whom much is given much is required. He shirked none of the responsibilities thrust upon him. They were, after all, what he had requested early in life. At nineteen, standing before the Holy Sepulcher in Jerusalem, he prayed that he be given "an intense life filled with Christian meaning." And it came to pass, perhaps more abundantly than he could have dreamed at that moment. As a university student he was attracted to science but soon realized that his professional vocation was philosophy. He sought truth—and to his satisfaction found it. For like St. Augustine he followed a dialectical pathway to two reasoned and reasonable conclusions: (A) that in its highest and purest form Truth is not an abstraction but God, and (B) that authentic philosophy is not simply the love of truth but the creative truth of God. To this foundation Marías added two more pillars: (C) that the foremost feature of human persons is not intelligence or rationality, important and necessary as they are, but rather the higher status of persons created in love, and (D) that personal annihilation is therefore unlikely. "The human person appears as a creature, whose reality is received but new and irreducible, needy and indigent, condemned to a closed empirical structure and called to mortality, yet consisting in incessant hope: a project which struggles with death. 'What' I am is mortal, but 'who' I am consists in aspiring to be immortal and not being able to imagine myself as not immortal, because my life is *radical*."

Now hear his concluding words on the matter: "*If we are obliged to accept a person as a 'creature', as a created being, then we would have to justify the sense of that person's annihilation. From this perspective, the survival of a person appears to be coherent with the form of reality that we have discovered in personhood. Thus, in order to reject what we have discovered we would have to offer good reasons for personal destruction.*

"*Stating the matter in this way makes it appear impossible to ignore it. Unless we prefer not to see that the human person is a reality entirely different from all others and that we abandon the need to ask the radical questions we call philosophy.*"

United in a gigantic philosophic continuum that spanned nearly an entire century and two lifetimes, Ortega and Marías said much to demonstrate the radical nature of human life, culminating with Marías' cited words affirming the likelihood that life transcends mortality precisely because it is radical in a sense unlike any other I encounter. **Therefore, unless we argue for a universe that operates at random, it does not make sense that lowest materiality should be indestructible but the highest reality we know of should be destined for annihilation.**

Part III:

The Immortal Narrative

8. The Passing of Soledad

We have witnessed some of the efforts by Ortega and Marías to rescue human reality from abstraction, animalism, genetics, and materiality. In doing so, we have been enabled to view human life in relief as both the radical reality that implicates all other realities, great and small, and as the person, male and female, in the actual modes and attributes of human life in this real world. Now we are prepared, as best we can be, to repeat the last of the fundamental questions raised at the beginning of this writing: what is our destiny? At several levels our inquiry took the form of a narrative. And in that mode, we shall begin this last section by telling the rest of Soledad's story and commenting on some of its implications:

Word reached us that Soledad has passed away. The reader will recall that her story was told in Ortega's writings and retold by Marías in his as a narrative illustration of the empirical theory of life. Hear now the rest of her story, which will serve as an introduction to the theme of immortality.

Friends tell us that one moment Soledad was as vibrant and charming as ever, and the next she was dead. Efforts to revive her failed, and if known, the cause of her death was not made public, only that it happened suddenly without warning. Her faithful and devoted lover, the man we have always known only as A, is inconsolable and wants nothing more than to join her in death.

Our sorrow is real, too, but naturally less than his. Our

friendship with both belongs largely to our youth. In later years our paths seldom crossed, and we know little about their life since our days with them long ago. Nor is it clear to us whether A's unconditional love for Soledad was ever fully reciprocated. She was the kind of woman who let herself be adored and men eagerly obliged. But it was always less certain whether in turn she loved them as much, if indeed at all. Great beauty sometimes partners with a stunted generosity of spirit. Every life has its secrets and contradictions. Did A live with the pain of her indifference or the happiness of her love? Did they marry each other or take separate life pathways? What episodes and adventures marked their mature years? And to whom does it matter? The further in time and affections from us death happens, the less intense the loss becomes. To strangers at an emotional remove Soledad's death and A's grief repeat the familiar story of human mortality and spiral of earthly life.

Hushed voices and pious truisms characterize funerals. But even the best of words seem as intrusive as they are necessary in the solemn atmosphere in which bad manners and humor are unthinkable. We tell one another that Death comes to all, as though sorrows multiplied were sorrows lessened. Pious words and solemn faces do not alleviate the suffering of the bereaved. Nor does collective grief really console us. For death does not happen abstractly and statistically to all, but privately and personally to each. Death is an event that requires words, but words are symbols and do not reach the core of grief. Yet for all its alien, impenetrable mystery every death is a foreshadowing of our own. This is why—always excepting the death of those close to us—we experience an indecent relief that we are spared to live another day. No wonder hearty appetites accompany wakes and funerals.

Absorbed in these strayed reflections and dressed in our somber best we pay our respects and offer condolences to the family and friends. There we see Soledad's familiar features as her beautifully attired body lies in state. Although time has left its mark on her features, her beauty remains. Indeed, the facial lines of private tensions are gone, and her relaxed face has regained its earlier perfection. Now it is as though paradoxically in death she had recaptured her youth. We recall her smile, eyes, gestures, laughter, vivacity, and the inimitable lilt of her voice that so charmed all who knew her. We half expect her to rise at any second and welcome us to the party she made of life.

But no, such happy images seem sacrilegious in these somber circumstances. Grieving has its own timeless traditions and protocols. With an effort we banish wayward thoughts as we stop for a moment to view her corpse. There is no movement, no life left in it, and we must not embellish our impressions as the ladies have done her hair and adorned her body. Soledad is no longer present, even though physically little about her appears to have changed except the unusual stillness and serenity that have come over her. We see her but can only wonder whether she sees us. She was always a woman of movement, excitement, surprise, joy, and zest who as though by magic knew how to rouse the dourest friends to laughter. But was her gaiety also a defense of her vulnerable tenderness? How can this still body be the much-admired woman to whom silence was an affront and idleness a waste of life?

The truth is hard to understand and even harder to take, and all the harder because we do not understand it. This may be Soledad, but not the one we knew. That Soledad is gone in a familiar yet mysterious way we acknowledge but do not really comprehend. Yet the fact is undeniable; before us forever at rest in the casket lies the visible evidence of her death. We take a deep breath and sternly caution our rebellious emotions to remain under control. It is a struggle. The feelings of many people saturate the funeral parlor, threatening to overwhelm our stoic determination to keep ours in check.

At the funeral service the priest recounts her virtues and speaks of Soledad rising to a better life in a better realm. Later we move in a solemn, black-clad procession to the adjacent cemetery. Now the casket is closed. We shall not see her again. Pebbles and dirt rattle the casket as it comes to rest in the tomb, and loved ones toss flowers and earth on it. "Ashes to ashes, dust to dust," the priest intones the ancient belittling words of mortal fate. We imagine Soledad lying in total darkness, for once unsmiling, for once and ever still and silent. But does she hear and perceive? The brighter life the priest described seems too removed to convince. It was a fabulous story, but things fabulous are the children of fable, and we struggle to reconcile the hopeful witness of our faith with the contradictory evidence that feeds our doubts.

Her casket and concealed body, we remind ourselves, are the real, visible, non-judgmental evidence, the phenomenological proof, as it were, that her life is over. We stifle a first impulse to reject the priestly words as pious sentimentality and side with the materialists who teach that the death of the body is also the death of Soledad. In search of consolation that faith does not offer at this hard moment, we begin a further consideration of the evidence before us. For analysis of evidence is also part of the dynamics of life, and perhaps the most human form. The history of humanity is the uneven progress into the invisible, symbolic realities of creation. Therefore, we cannot limit ourselves to surface phenomenological evidence; second and subsequent probes are a higher province of humans. In the presence of mortality we must strive all the harder to retain and justify our living humanity.

Here indeed lies bodily proof that life is over for Soledad. But a more penetrating analysis rescues us from morbidity. For the same evidence is the most compelling proof that Soledad was never her body, for it is still present; never her bodily chemistry or biology, for all the elements necessary for chemical or biological life, if such they were, are still intact; nor did her life reside in the intricate neural and cerebral organs that received and transmitted sensory impressions, for these organs still exist. What, then, has happened to prevent her bodily processes from reviving spontaneously or with the help of medical stimulation? Simply but mysteriously her life has departed her body—or is it that her life has expelled her body? Either of which argues that Soledad was more than her body, and that by analogy so must we be also.

But if as we discovered in Ortegan philosophy, "my" life, the life of each of us, is the radical, or root, reality in which all other perceivable realities are rooted, including my body and its mortal condition, then the first logical deduction that we can make is not that the corpse we still call "Soledad" proves that her life has ceased to be, but instead that her life has ceased to animate her body. Her relationship to it has changed. Thus if Soledad was never her mortal body, then we cannot say with certainty that her life has ceased to be, only that the relationship of body and life in her case has been altered.

This logic is perplexing, and we do not fully trust our reasoning. Therefore, let us take a different rational track. Death is something that Soledad experienced in her life. For we saw earlier that mortality is inherently and unavoidably a feature of life. The common euphuism we repeat to soften the jarring fact of death turns out be entirely fitting. For not only does death itself—though often not the circumstances—now appear to be less brutal than we commonly assume, but also that it consists not of a cessation but a separation. Her body is here but Soledad "has passed away." Or to think of it in yet another way, she is who she always has been, undefined, boundless, and radically inclusive. She is still Soledad and her circumstance, which includes her body, only now it is circumstantially in her life in a different way and as a changed component. A conclusion occurs to us: *Soledad's corpse, which at first appeared to be incontrovertible proof that she has ceased to be, from another perspective is equally strong evidence against the cessation of her being.* Logically, and thus possibly, her life may continue, for we have not by any means proved that it ceased with her death. We are beset by an old, recurring thought: as we get closer to life's deepest truths, they become increasingly paradoxical and mystifying to our linear Western minds.

Our skeptical spirit, still clinging to ancient limitations, counters that neither have we proved that her life continues, for we see no evidence of it. But neither could we see it before her death, we respond, just as we could not see her love or happiness, or occasional sorrow, only its effects and our uncertain surmises. In both cases, life has proved to be an ineffable reality from a physical, materialistic perspective, *not a thing, not an object, not anything material, but an immeasurable reality of an entirely different sort.* The two perspectives converge and intersect at the moment of death, and both make their appeal at Soledad's funeral. But being inconclusive, we cannot conclusively favor either at the moment. So let us bid Soledad a fond farewell and continue our reasoning elsewhere accompanied by the following thoughts.

9. Justifying Mortality

This segment deserves some precautionary comments. To begin with, the uncertainties of life and the hope of immortality are insufficient reasons to disdain our mortal time in this world. In fact, we alternate between clinging to life here and now in mortal form and dismissing it as unworthy in two ways: (1) in comparison to the immortal life to come, as many believe, or (2) in view of the total cessation of life that others suppose.

Yet mortal life clearly has a purpose and a justification of its own. The dim hues or bright colorings of our views of death condition our life in this world, regardless of its relative brevity. (And can we not think of it as brief because we have an innate sense of immortality?) Both competing views—cessation of being or continuation of life—may induce us to exaggerate. Over the ages some martyrs have been so eager to end earthly days and begin their heavenly life that they scorned their time here as altogether unworthy and went to their death singing songs of joy. In grotesque cases parents have even killed their children with the specious justification that their sinless innocence surely earns them a place in paradise. On the other hand, there are others for whom there is no basis for morality and the devastating chaos this leads to is of immediate concern only if they are its victims. In a wider, impersonal context they are indifferent to social and political devastation. For them mortality justifies immorality.

Yet the meanest man that lives reveals a dignity in death that in life he may never have shown, or we may not have acknowledged. Crime and villainy may be his monstrous legacy. But even if his life was a moral outrage, his death suddenly reveals not only who he was meant to be but also the image of who he could have been. This circumstance reminds us again of something we often forget: that life, even a corrupted life, preserves an ineradicable worth. Misuse and abuse of gifts may horrify us, but only because we sense in such debased persons the original splendor and promise of their creation.

From a believer's perspective, our personal susceptibility to error and misuse of gifts prompts a logical question: if by an act of effusive divine love we were created for undying life, then why did the Creator subject us first to mortality instead of placing us directly in paradisiacal immortality? Did he commit a colossal blunder? A first response, which is compatible with several religions, is that humanity had its chance in the Edenic Paradise and failed miserably. But we also read that the earthly destiny of mankind was not to remain in the Edenic Paradise in the first place; instead by divine mandate humans were to multiply and dominate the earth. Nevertheless, in this paradigm mortality and expulsion from the Garden are understood as punishment for human sin. The subsequent history of humanity then becomes a tragic drama of human suffering and uncertain personal redemption, which again begs the question: if God had the power to save his creation and rescue his creatures—all his creation and creatures—then why did he not do so, and do so quickly? Surely upon seeing their children threatened by malevolent beings, earthly parents would rush in immediately to rescue them from harm. Something seems amiss in the conventional paradigm.

St. Peter wrote that to God a day is like a thousand years, and a thousand years like a day. No doubt this is true, but primarily symbolically so; we do not live and think in such temporal spans. To us a day is a human day, and while we can acknowledge the Petrine formula, we still must live our life one day at a time, and each one is like a miniature lifetime. This means that before we can examine evidence for immortality we must make a better effort to justify mortal life in this world and in the kind of time we understand. The imperative set forth at the beginning of this book still holds: what we accept on faith, we have a duty to complement as best we can with reason.

Earthly mortality with all its agony and redemptive uncertainties may be understood and justified from at least two perspectives:

(1) if we had been placed in the immortal paradise with absolute assurance and factual certainty of everlasting life we would have no faith, nor need of it, only unspoken confidence, just as ordinarily we take for granted the air we breathe and the ground we stand on. They are too common to be commented.

With inspired insight St. Paul wrote ages ago that faith is the substance of things hoped for, the evidence of things not seen. How right he was, for like love, faith presupposes the unseen and the unrealized. And also like love, it is selective, at once choosing and rejecting, and is therefore "elegant" in the primary meaning of the word. The substance and the hope of unseen things are not random, promiscuous bindings to unworthy things strewn helter-skelter but links to those essential realities and people we need in order to live fully, that is, in supernatural fullness. This why I consider faith to be another form of love, and as like to it as a twin. It appears humble but in reality it is majestic in its efficacy. For like Jacob's Ladder, it forms a luminous channel between the lowest mortals and highest Heaven. Through it flow in private streams pleas and petitions, gifts and graces, instruction and enlightenment.

As I wrote above, had we been placed directly in Paradise we would have no hope or faith. In a paradoxical sense we could say that we would be "hopeless" and "faithless," not in the forlorn sense these terms have in this lower, incomplete life, but in the meaning of satiety, the possession of all we could wish for. For as St. Paul also points out, *we do not hope for what we already have*, though we may appreciate and desire it. Both faith and hope imply distance and separation; they are the gifts by which we love and stand strong in separation from the object of hope. Both are heroic, steadfast assurances of our everlasting destiny. For they link us to realities that thereby become ours, but though ours are not yet fully in our possession. Hope and faith are not lesser sops granted as compensation to lower creatures, but perhaps our highest qualities, to judge by the lavish praise and reward they earn in sacred writings. Nevertheless, their place is here and now in this world even though they culminate and assume other forms, outcomes, and revelations in the next.

Our life story, or drama, in this world consists of episodes, events, and experiences. Earlier I described human life as "eventful," and because living is a futuristic, anticipatory task, as "eventual," We mark our life by events and live in their expectation, that is, by what we do and what happens to us as we do. Perils lurk like predators along our pathway. Living is dangerous, and danger is hidden in the word "experience" itself. "Ex-" means "from" and the next component "per-" so eroded that we barely recognize it, is "peril." The final element determines the nominal, verbal, or adjectival form of the word.

We learn from experience, as the saying goes, meaning literally that we learn by living through its perils. And most of us would agree that these are the most unforgettable and unforgiving lessons. Dullards may not learn much from books and teachers, but by common consensus the greatest fools are those who do not learn from experience.

(2) We wonder at first why error and peril should be mentioned at all in the happy context of immortal life. *But without the earthly experience we would not be ourselves but another kind of creature.* If we entered Paradise directly we would have no memories or projects to develop and probably no sense of purpose or intentionality. It would be as though we were adults without the formative, learning stages and memories of childhood, or, conversely, children without an equally necessary image of adulthood. Earthly life allows us to grow, to learn, to project, to plan, to correct, to look prospectively ahead and retrospectively behind.

It is a religious platitude to wish the deceased "eternal rest." But no wish could be drearier, no sentence deadlier, than everlasting idleness and stasis. Perhaps it is the state of being we call Hell. For we were created to create, made to make, given life so as to forge more abundant life.

We commonly claim to long for a life of ease and peace of mind. But do we really? Our fondest daydreams may be fantasies of idle hours in peaceful, paradisiacal surroundings. But greater souls remind us constantly that this minimalist ideal is neither our personal nor collective destiny. And they show us the way by abandoning their fate so as to create their destiny. No social ambition drives them, though it may be an adjunct of their drive. Nor can we assign their eccentric urge to economic or sociological factors, though these may affect their course or even conceal their motives. The modern notion that environmental conditions alone can explain both the destructive lawlessness of some people and the constructive drive in others is intellectually slothful and suspect. For the latter group it is too personal a quest to obey the abstract laws that rule abstract things. They may suffer hunger in their quest, but a deeper hunger drives them. It is comparable to a love without a lover or the phantom pain of an amputated limb. The shapers of human fortunes are not born for the calm and the quiet but for the storm and the battle. They are always apt to disturb and anger placid people who think the world is good enough as it is or would be if only it could be again as it used to be. These shapers of the world personify the wild card of chance that breaks old patterns and restores freedom. They come unpredictably out of nowhere to turn the world on its ear and set it spinning toward untried alternatives. The settled world patterns are never safe with these people. They exhibit symptoms of an incurable and incurably benign virus that reshapes the world. And if given a chance to live, any human infant may be infected with it. Of old it received its name: divine discontent.

It is a sign that we were not born to remain in our first phase. Stagnant life is archaic, and the archaic does not prosper. It is a reversal of life and contrary to its condition. Everything human is essentially futuristic. Our eyes are located on our face looking forward in time and space, not on the back of our head looking backward to what already was and for that reason cannot be again. Otherwise, probably we would have been created in mature, finished form, condemned never to grow or age, never to understand the past or future, never to know the human condition, and forever confined to a futureless world of stasis, in short to be a different kind of creature.

What are we to make of these irrepressible and unpredictable humans bent on restructuring the world? Obviously in the first instance, we must realize that the world in its circumstance and we in our human condition are not finished and fully accomplished. We were not created to remain on idyllic desert islands. In the words of poet Robert Frost, "we have promises to keep and miles to go before we sleep." From all we know about the telluric and geological stages of the earth within the vaster evolution of the Universe itself, it seems reasonable to think that to be susceptible to change is to be inextricably committed to it. As scientist-theologian Teilhard de Chardin describes it, "Under the commonplace envelope of things and of all our purified and salvaged efforts, a New Earth is being slowly engendered." Change and growth remain the general creative imperatives. Or to put it in simpler language, the created Universe is dynamic, and so necessarily is created life. Dynamism occurs as disruption of the set and settled, but from disruption comes design, from chaos emerges new order, from old man is born the new man.

The human person appears as a created being, whose reality is given and received and called to mortality, yet consisting in enduring hope of a greater life, a life that contends with death. I am I and my circumstance, and if I do not save it, I do not save myself, or know salvation. To put it another way, I am the sum of all I have loved, done, suffered, and lived. And so I remain, inseparable, indivisible from, yet changing with, my changing circumstance, in this life and perhaps forever. We shall still be ourselves in immortality, or I should say, more ourselves, more truly who we are. This means that we shall not forego or forget our mortal life. Instead we shall surely be grateful for our remembered life with all its lessons, loves, experiences, and sufferings. To live again, or better, to continue living, is not to become a different being oblivious to the sum of circumstances but to continue to achieve the plenitude of who I was always destined to be. I shall be the same, only more than the same. To be forgiven for my mistakes, my sins, for what I have done wrong or wrongly, is to see those experiences changed from negative to positive, from bad to good, from decay to edification, from evil to good. I must change so as to remain myself and thus become more truly myself.

10. Immortality: The Converging Evidence

With Ortega we learned that "my" life, the life of each person, is incomparably distinct from any other reality we know of. In my life, and only in my life, I encounter all things real, unreal, and quasi-real: objects, other persons, my own body, transcendent realities, realities that were, realities that may become, events past and possible, impossibilities, fictions, truths, untruths, and death itself all occur in my life. Life is the stage on which the drama of creation becomes visible and actual. And the main role is mine. In summary, everything that has a presence and can make an impression presents itself and makes its impression on me only in my life. In all their being, plain or problematic, things appear only in my life. For this reason, the reason that is unlike any other we know of, Ortega called "my life" the "radical reality."

In turn, with Marías we examined the ways we are actually installed in life and how life unfolds empirically, that is, as we live it experientially. The antecedents of my bodily being—

genetics, heredity, ancestry—condition but are not sufficient to account for the person that I am. This means that although I have an especial association with my body, I am not identical to it. Instead, my life appears as creation, a reality that cannot be reduced to, or explained by, anything or anybody else. The death of my body is completely understandable; the physical "what" that I am perishes, but to the "who" that I am, the person who engages in understanding, who executes the perception, and who plays the lead role in the drama of life, my personal death is formally unthinkable. In order to imagine death, mine or that of anyone, I must in some sense be there before, during, and after death as a witness to the event. This means, I repeat, that I am not identical with my mortal body and not reducible to it. My life, though not my body, appears to me as something absolute and indestructible, and my death an experience that I encounter as the living person that I am.

Here we confront what now appears to be humanity's greatest and most enduring error: the assumption that my life is my physical body, and as the first corollary that mortality, the destruction of my body, is also the cessation of my life. According to the scientific law of the indestructability as modified in the twentieth century, matter cannot be destroyed, though it can pass from one state to another; since Einstein we know that matter may be transformed into energy, or vice versa. Because the law coheres seamlessly with the philosophy of radical reality that we have examined in a dual way in this writing and in equal measure with the Judeo-Christian doctrines of immortality, it is logical and reasonable to apply it also to human life, and probably to all life. But the latter concept is another story that is not mine to tell.

Therefore, if we were to take it upon ourselves to argue that human life is an exception to the general law of indestructibility, as many do implicitly or knowingly, then we would be obliged to justify the annihilation of the highest creation with the lowest of evidence and do so against the arrayed forces of the three streams of human reason. Failure in the dialectical skirmish, like Don Quixote's joust with the windmills, would be predictable, a failure that is not a defeat but really a backhanded assertion of life. There are battles we must lose in order to win greater victories. The extended application of the Law of Indestructability implies a corollary: *as mortals we live already in immortality*. This realization presents us with a decisive moral choice, either to live life as we choose to be forever and for which death is not an embarrassment, or to spend our life in a series of harmful expediencies to which death can offer only remorse.

We have reached the climactic moment in our philosophical narrative of human life. Now we see before us the grand confluence of three streams of Western thought. Judeo-Christian Theology, the Philosophy of Radical Reality, and the Scientific Law of Indestructibility converge to affirm with triple force the imperishability of personal reality. Were proof available to us of flaws in the cosmic structure and exceptions to the laws and principles that govern it, then we might have justifiable cause to doubt personal indestructibility. Finding no such cause and no proven reason to doubt it, we can say with reasoned and reasonable certainty that *personal life cannot be utterly annihilated*. **As the great pagan poet Horace wrote ages ago, "I shall not wholly die." This means that I may live in the assurance that I shall remain indestructibly who I am and shall be so before and after mortality. My body dies so that I may live more fully by this release from mortality. Therefore,**

religious faith is also justified and reaffirmed. The evidence for immortality is also the assurance that those I love, those I shall come to love, and those who love or have loved me share unending life with me. For what is surely true for me must assuredly be true for all.

Were mortality our final destiny, then our individual death would be more than our solitary demise. For if my life is the radical reality in which appear all other realities in structural and dynamic order and significance, then would not death mean the dissolution of an entire universe? Would not each death, if absolute, mean the destruction not merely of a solitary person but of whole Cosmos with it? And can we not glimpse in this vast personalized structure the unimaginable possibilities inherent in the creation of each person?

In it seems reasonable to think that this many-splendored indestructibility of life is also a way to understand and clarify several puzzling matters in Holy Writ. For example, if one accepts that evil is personified as diabolical beings that work wrathfully to thwart the will of God and bring suffering to mankind—and not incidentally, to themselves—then why, we ask, does God not simply annihilate the life of these malevolent creatures and eliminate a major source of human suffering? In like manner, but at a far remove and from another perspective, why did God order or encourage the Hebrews to eliminate various peoples in the conquest of the Promised Land? The ethnic cleansing in the second example is especially gruesome to modern sensitivities. But by what we have just said about created reality, the apparent destruction was less than real. For if it were total and eternal, then would it not mean that their creation would have been a mistake or error of creation? The hostile tribes died, or at least a portion of them did, but the reasoning holds: their death was not their destruction. What God creates he does not destroy but transforms.

Likewise, the Fallen Angels are created beings, created for ever, and by the same law apparently cannot simply be annihilated so long as the Law of indestructability holds. For mortality, a phenomenon and an experience but not fully a reality, ceases to haunt humanity by death itself, which liberates created beings to continue their immortal life. I repeat, continue, for to insist on a point made earlier, we live already in eternity. These are examples, as I think, of ways in which alternate ways of reaching truth can bolster and clarify theological teachings.

Here I acknowledge anecdotal accounts of persons apparently or really deceased who have revived to resume their mortal life. But I do not offer them as proof of continuing life after death. Not that I categorically doubt the veracity of all reported cases of revival. Nevertheless, for two principal reasons I choose to exclude them: first, because many of the accounts are sketchy and perhaps apocryphal. I have witnessed no cases of resurrection myself, and the ones I know of have been retold by an uncertain number of people before reaching me. Stories grow in the telling, and the more people who repeat them, the greater the variance from fact is likely to become. But the second reason for the exclusion is the weightier. Most such accounts cannot be scientifically or medically verified as authentic cases. It seems likely that in a great many cases inexpert witnesses mistook deep coma or profound unconsciousness for death. I have no reason to doubt reports that some persons on the verge of eternity were told they must go back to complete tasks or to live a better life, but neither do I have any objective way of knowing whether in other cases the message originated in a source beyond them, was produced by their own traumatized consciousness, or was simply fabricated for attention. The accounts themselves are intriguing, but beyond that I see no reason to include them in this book. Defective proof is worse than no proof.

But now we come to a different problem. We have seen how the three main avenues of inquiry—Theology, Science, and Philosophy—have converged to support the general premise of the indestructibility of life. But does anyone want to go there and personally verify the truth? We know the usual answer: given a choice between here and the Hereafter, most of us would choose to stay here. There are several obvious but very different reasons for our reluctance. First, are we fully convinced that life really continues as an "Afterlife"? Even if it does, the term is revealing and demeaning. After our busy earthly life of food, drink, play, entertainment, love, marriage, sex, parenthood, success, failure, strife and struggle is over, we begin an "after" life, like a musical encore or coda after our mortal melody has ended.

Additionally, instead of our busy agenda in this life, the main feature in the next seems to be either "eternal rest" or everlasting singing, both of which to many of us are only marginally and sporadically appealing. What about those who enjoy quiet conversation, scientific research, or philosophic contemplation? Otherwise, it is not clear whether life in that realm offers the legitimate pleasures we enjoyed in this plane, much less prohibited ones always condemned yet immemorially practiced. There will be better activities, people hasten to assure us. But exactly what are they and are they really activities we shall enjoy? Are there food, drink and other physical joys in that life, or must we forego such delights altogether? We desire Heaven, but to tell the truth, most of us dread going there.

Second, we must first die in order to begin our immortal life, at least from the conventional point of view, and the transition often comes accompanied by considerable pain, sadness, suffering, and bother not only in our life but also in the lives of our family and loved ones, as we saw in the death and funeral of Soledad. It seems that there is seldom a convenient "deathday." As the old Romans said, death comes when it will at an "uncertain hour" of its choosing. Third, there are the awful options of Heaven and Hell. Which shall be our personal destination? We hope there are enough positives in our life to merit a Divine nod of approval. But we also remember the negatives, confessed or concealed, that may damn us. We have confessed our faith and said our prayers, but did we do so sincerely or with indifference and unconscious hypocrisy? If we are Catholic we understand that there may be an intermediate stop in Purgatory, but its traditional images resemble a suburb of Hell more than an outskirt of Heaven.

Fourth, it may have been relatively easy to leave this "vale of tears" in former times when life was brutally harsh, but for many people today earthly life has vastly greater appeal. The truth is, we feel sorry for the dead as they must leave the "good life" behind to begin an uncertain and possibly austere afterlife. Although we mechanically repeat that "they are in a better place," we prefer to avoid it ourselves as long as possible.

But perhaps the greatest problem, among the several mentioned above, is that although we acknowledge our immortal destiny, we have not given it much thought, mostly because we have no well-defined frame of reference and only scant, metaphorical teaching in religious writings. Whether true or not, someone has said that Jesus talked more about money than about Heaven. No wonder then that we have not tried to imagine what the content of our personal life will be like beyond mortality. How can we imagine something so different from what we experience in this life? Or does it indeed differ as much as we think? We cannot comprehensively imagine Heaven, but it seems reasonable and necessary to try. For what we do not or cannot imagine we cannot realistically desire. Our conventional concepts of immortal life are short on detail and probably long on error. The truth is we need someone to give us a more humanized description of Heaven. But in lieu of such a person, I offer as a conclusion the following skeletal comments for your consideration.

Conclusion:

What is Time? Who is God?

For several reasons, some of which we saw earlier, most of us dread immortality nearly as much as we desire it. Even time itself which at first seems so clear, becomes baffling in an everlasting context. According to the words of a popular Christian hymn, time in immortal life is endless, of course, yet we still interpret it in the same linear, segmented terms we knew in this world:

> When we've been there ten thousand
> years, bright shining as the sun,
>
> We've no less days to sing God's praise
> than when we'd first begun.

At first it seems a trifling matter that leaves the message intact and theologically praiseworthy. But in a larger context we discover problems that affect the very idea of heavenly happiness.

First of all, the image of endless praising and singing, like an everlasting church service, hints of an altered personal condition. It suggests that we are no longer our normal selves as we understand normal but have changed, or been changed, into a different kind of creature, perhaps only a fleshless, unsubstantial spirit that the ancients described as a "shade." If we are honest about it, we fear that in the Hereafter the Divine Powers may change us into pious but unrecognizable beings and that we could cease to be ourselves, or at least without control over ourselves. The idea of resting or congregating eternally in endless praise of Deity is only a step or two removed from the Buddhist dogma of Nirvana, which in my limited understanding of Buddhism means that after repeated earthly reincarnations our life culminates in the reabsorption of our being and its sufferings into the cosmic ocean of life. Thus, if Western unbelievers fear annihilation at death, the faithful have a vague dread of alteration. Both have in common a fear of ceasing to be who they are, though in different ways.

The second reason is the problem of time itself in the Hereafter. Debates about time in this world continue among the so-called "Presentist," "Eternalist" or "Block Universe," and "Growing Past" philosophers of time. In an earlier book, *The Unknown God*, I wrote on these and other time theories, including J.M.E McTaggert's seminal essay "The Unreality of Time," but it would take us too far afield to go into them in this writing. My interest here is time in this context and how it may relate to happiness in the woefully-named "Afterlife." For happiness remains the ultimate hope of mankind in this life or anywhere else. It begins, however, with what I hold to be two categories or levels of time in this world. I call them Kairotic and Chronological time.

I call on Shakespeare to introduce them in Act IV of *Julius Caesar:*

> There is a tide in the affairs of men,
> which taken at the flood,
> leads on to fortune. Omitted,
> all the voyage of their life
> is bound in shallows and in miseries.
> On such a full sea are we now afloat,
> and we must take the current when it serves,
> or lose our ventures.

Shakespeare's magnificent language refers symbolically to a special kind of time which the Greeks called <u>Kairos</u>, in contrast to <u>Chronos</u>, or cosmic time, personified in Greek mythology as Cronos the Devourer. Kairos is personal or personalized time, specifically, the opportune time for action. It is qualitative time, whereas <u>Chronos</u> is quantitative time, the steady, featureless time we measure in hours, minutes, hours, days, weeks and years. We mark off time by arbitrary segments; a day could have thirty hours if we so decided; an hour could be eighty minutes, and a year could be as long as we declared it to be.

Cosmic time is seamlessly indivisible; the segments—seconds, minutes, weeks, years—are human divisions we attribute to time. Kairos consists of extraordinary moments of uncertain duration but which tend to be of brief intensity. Passion, triumph, and happiness soon culminate and subside, and we begin their pursuit anew. Kairos consists of personal peaks and valleys that may lead to pain and peril, but also possible happiness and fulfillment. Patience is a match for Chronos, but passion is suited to Kairos.

Because the Judeo-Christian Scriptures in large part consist of human narratives rather than formal doctrines and premises, they describe many kairotic moments. "For everything there is a season and a time to every purpose under the heaven: a time to be born, and a time to die . . ." Kairos also has theological implications. It is the "fullness of time" when God acts in a mighty way. In Catholic liturgy it is the concentrated, enriched time of the Eucharistic reenactment.

Life is a matter of time, the form of being that human life takes in the world. But it appears configured in two modes, externally chronological and intimately kairotic. Human life is not primarily chronological but kairotic, discontinuously molded and intensified by events, episodes, moods, acts, loves, animosities, hopes, triumphs, and failures. As far as we can judge by appearances, material things exist in chronological time, while personal life is essentially kairotic. But not entirely. Our mastery of kairotic time is incomplete; it surges, dips, and runs dry. In varying degrees life consists of a tension between kairotic time we possess as persons and chronological time that possesses us as impersonal, material things.

Chronological time passes implacably, or appears to, devouring our life as the Titan Cronos, or Father Time, devoured his children. But here is the point I was coming to: though itself episodic and soon spent, kairotic time lingers nevertheless in the impress of memory and the pregnant anticipation of fulfillment, success, and happiness. It offers the hope of a desirable future. We do not possess the future, and despite Shakespeare's words, have no assurance of triumph in our ventures. The tide may indeed sweep us on to victory or smash our schemes. But at least kairotic time allows us to live on credit and place a hopeful claim on future happiness.

Kairos is the spacious, nearly measureless time of infancy and childhood. But as we live, expending it in personal events, games, and projects, the fund of personal kairotic time dwindles and impersonal chronological time appears progressively to replace it. Since kairotic times seems to be characterized by fullness, and chronological time by fleetingness, time appears to accelerate proportionally with age as it becomes ever more chronological. We all sense and comment on the temporal acceleration but attribute it to a fundamental illusion. Perhaps it is no illusion at all but a real temporal phenomenon.

This brings up the question of alternate immortalities. Will it be possible one day to avoid death altogether and achieve immortality in this world and time? In the United States and the United Kingdom techniques are being developed to repair eroded human telomeres and thus extend life indefinitely. Robotic enhancement or replacement of failing bodily organs to achieve earthly immortality is another theoretical alternative. Lastly, despite strong moral aversions in the West, but not necessarily in some non-Western nations, it may prove possible to clone humans. But would such a clone be a person at all? More to the point, would it be the same person I am, or a simulacrum, a duplicate <u>who</u>, or merely an extraneous <u>what</u> that physically resembles me? Would personal memory, awareness, and conscience exist in both bodies? And could they enter into conflict with each other?

These and many other problems devolve on the exclusiveness of personhood and the reality of time. Consider a speculative example of the latter. If the fullness of time, what we have called Kairotic time, characterizes immortal time in the next world and a diminishing portion of life in this world, what would this mean for the still hypothetical eternal earthly life when Kairotic time is exhausted and totally replaced by chronological time? Could it mean the "emptiness of time," that is, time for nothing, time so accelerated that there would not be enough of it to complete projects. Perhaps life would become an everlasting paradoxical frustration: though undying, we would be too rushed to live and always "short of time." Life would become an endless rush of failures and ultimately an intolerable burden. It could be one definition of Hell. Who would not tire of such a life and long to see it end so that real immortality might begin? Haste and speed resemble sin. The Saints never appear hurried yet are always on time. On the other hand, Satan describes his restless life as ". . . going to and fro in the earth and walking up and down in it."

These and other questions are rooted in our ignorance of time in general. We have no real knowledge of what time is—or even the certainty that it exists at all, as McTaggert pointed out in his controversial essay—yet we proceed as though we did. We look to Science for knowledge of what time is, but it does not tell us very much beyond the interval between events or the precision of measurement to the nano-second of minutes, hours, days, and years. Yet we know that these precise intervals and units are not time itself but simply calculations based ultimately on the rotations and revolutions of the earth, cosmic expansion, the vibrations of atoms, or, commonly, the movement of celestial bodies. Taking the theories of relativity into consideration, I once wrote that *time is the duration of space and space is the fullness of time.* Admittedly the description means that each dimension is defined by the other and tells little else except that perhaps these twin dimensions cannot be separated, at least not at this stage of human science.

Western people assume that time is linear in this life and the next, but science has detected no "arrow of time" to confirm it. Other cultures have taught that time is circular, among them the Classical Mayans and Greeks. The latter considered the circle to be the perfect figure and in keeping with that perfection time was thought to occur as *palingenesia*, a Greek term that means "a return to the same," in other words, the completion of a giant temporal circle. If this teaching was based on a correct assumption—and we have no valid scientific proof to contradict it that I know of—then the famous and feared "end of time," as understood in a linear sense in the West, may indicate the completion of a cosmic time circle. It leaves us to wonder whether there have been previous temporal circles and others to come.

Many mystics over the ages have said that time is an illusion. But if time is linear and singular in mode in the immortal world and we experience it there as we think we do here, then happiness in that realm becomes problematic. For there is not enough time to do and experience all that would be needed to achieve full happiness. It would be wrong to say even as immortal persons we have "all the time in the world." For linear time elapses, passes, and moves on eon after eon, as we saw in words to the hymn. And what of past time? What of the missed encounters? The happy sessions we could have had with loved ones? The lovely scenes we never saw? The friends we never met? The music we never heard?

Furthermore, the very memory of happy times we experienced takes on a melancholy hue in our memories. "Where are the snows of yesteryears?" asks the poet with ineffable yearning for the joys, loves, beauties, and pleasures of the long ago. Many poets have written of the sweet sadness of recalling the happy days of yore. After "ten thousand years," as the hymn describes, would our melancholy nostalgia be multiplied by ages of accumulated happy memories? Perhaps we do not remember things there in the same way we do here as mortals. But if not, it would mean that our being has been modified, as we feared, and deprived of a key feature of our humanity. The noble pagan poet Lucretius said that without our memories we could not be the person we are.

Let us consider another paradisiacal dilemma that has a connection to a common earthly experience. We cannot and dare not imagine a Heaven devoid of beauty. It is easy for us to think of breathtaking vistas, lovely skies, and dramatic horizons. But earthly beauty eventually becomes commonplace. Beauty too often seen becomes beauty ignored. Familiarity does not necessarily breed contempt, as the saying goes, but indifference. Those who live among mountains or on seashores eventually barely seem to take notice of them. When everything is granted, everything is taken for granted. Beauty makes its greatest impact at first encounter. Later it sinks to the ordinary. I say all this to wonder how our enthusiasm for paradisiacal beauty will or can remain fresh and stimulating.

This brings up a problematic alternative to our common idea of linear time in the Hereafter: the concept of temporal simultaneity, as Boethius (480-524) taught. We could call it the fullness of time, or personal access to all time and thus to every age and time. Just as we have local freedom in space and may, in principle, return as often as we desire to the same place, or many places, as our earthly life permits, so instead of our present restricted temporal freedom which allows us only the freedom to go only forward toward what we call the future, complete temporal simultaneity would permit us to visit any time, age, event, person, or experience as often as we might wish, including those which for lack of time or opportunity we could not experience in this mortal segment of life. In this world we say that time waits for no man, but in the next it may wait for everyone.

But despite its appealing features, the concept of simultaneity also presents enigmas. Some modern philosophers of time argue that since the advent of relativity theories the same event will be seen as occurring at different times according to the relative locations of viewers and that the concept of simultaneity is therefore invalid. But in response, may we not reason that simultaneity of time must also be the simultaneity of space, since it seems impossible, as I said earlier, to separate time and space? If we agree that in immortality we shall not be limited in space, then the theory of relative distance, and indeed distance itself—a mortal imposition born of limitation—is rendered invalid. For it would mean that in the fullness of life and time we are not localized in one space and confined to a single perspective but simultaneously present in all space and all perspectives in space-time.

The concept of simultaneity, as Boethius conceived it and as others have amended it, continues to be debated. For present purposes I have gone as far as prudence allows, and I remind the reader that all I have said on the topic is born of our common perplexity and probability, not absolute certainty. I add only that without a similar doctrine of temporal simultaneity, the whole question of human happiness in Heaven seems to me to be an open and unresolved theological question that may have no resolution in this mortal realm. To say so categorically would be to repeat the error of erecting prohibitive borders that supposedly no mind can cross. Surely experience has taught us enough to disregard human pronouncements about what we can and cannot know in the future.

I cannot leave these speculations without some brief comments on the topic of Deity. There is an immemorial debate with many branching lines and subtopics and a history older than the theory of simultaneity revisited above. Many of these may be subsumed in three general questions to which I shall limit myself here. First, does God exist at all? Second, did God create the Universe and mankind? And third, does he involve himself in Creation and therefore in time and the affairs of humanity? I have considered these and related questions in other writings. Here I touch on those that at the moment seem to be the most compelling.

To the first question I begin by saying that a theory of human life implies a related theory or theology of Deity. To the first question about the existence of God, we must answer no. Neither God nor persons <u>exist</u>; they <u>live</u> instead. Existence and life are two radically different modes of being and vastly different realities. As we saw in the earlier sections of this writing, my life is the radical reality in which all other realities and existences appear to me in my life. This means, as I see it, that the fundamental, sustaining reality of our life is personal, not merely existential in the secondary manner of sticks, stones and bones. Does God exist? Heaven forbid! God surely lives as we live, only more so, and in life, personal and divine, we live and move and have our being, understanding, reasoning, loving, and aspiring to greater life. This means that far from being the fixed, existent, immovable Principle of pagan thought—and by pagan contamination of certain lines of Christian theology—that sustains the Cosmos in existential modes, God lives, and by living acts dynamically within his creation not merely to sustain it but to guide it to expansive plenitude and fulfillment in the universe or multiverse he has created for that multi-dimensional expansion. Otherwise, we must wonder, shall a person, whether human or divine, build a house and refuse to set foot in it? Shall God create a Universe for himself, adorn it with his creatures and works, but choose to dwell elsewhere? Do we then exist in a God-free Universe, a polite way of saying a godless one? The idea is not plausible by any criteria I know of. For if Deity is absent or unimaginably remote from us, then all our Religions, Sciences, and Philosophies may be fanciful figments of collective human delirium, the laws of Science could be arbitrarily fickle and undependable, the prayers of believers over the ages would have fallen on a deaf, unheeding Cosmos, and Truth would be a chimera, not a divine person, as St. Augustine taught.

Many modern people are profoundly skeptical, which is a belief like any other save for its sterility: in engenders nothing. The fact that millions of persons have come to doubt all but the scientific postulates of our tripartite civilization—Theology, Philosophy, and Science—is an ominous reminder of how close we are to the general collapse of supra-natural culture.

Therefore, just as persons surely are not existential beings, neither does it seem theologically proper to think of God as a Perfected Person. Should we not say with fuller reverence and love that God is <u>Perfect</u> but not <u>Perfected</u> because his life is not over and never will be? By implication I mean that as a person God is dynamically at work, adding to his creation, alive in his Universe, and specifically present in the world with his people, correcting their mistakes, looking to their welfare, establishing the conditions for happiness, and ever creating and anticipating more life. The root of the word "perfect" is the Latin <u>factum,</u> a past participle meaning "done," "finished," or "completed." God is obviously not done, but still doing, still working, still creating, still perfecting. It seems more reasonable to say that he is Perfect, not Perfected, and neither is his work; he is not through with his people, not with his creatures, not with his world, not with his Universe, and above all not with Himself. The immortal narrative is not concluded. Perhaps it is only beginning.

Finally, as "radical" beings in the circumstantial sense that we have explored and outlined in this inquiry, are we not pushed to the conclusion that each life, beginning with each their own, is an entire, immeasurable Cosmos in which all reality is rooted, specifically meaning all the realities each of us knows, experiences, confronts, and deals with, and no less those we only suspect, or which comprise a much greater and variable body of ignorance? And must we not reasonably conclude, therefore, that the destruction and disappearance of human life in the absolute, final, and unappealable manner taught by skeptics, abortionists, and disbelievers would be the annihilation of an entire universe of infinite pluralities and possibilities we call a human person? Have we not yet learned that reality always turns out to be greater than we know? In the light of what we have discovered, does not Protagoras' ancient saying, "Man is the measure of all things," take on ever more hopeful and majestic meanings?

These, then, are what seem to me to be coherent and reasonable ways of considering the likelihood of personal immortality. Probably they will not move, much less persuade, hardened skeptics who in the name of enlightenment deny humanity's everlasting hope. In their case it will take a greater illumination to pierce their darkness. But perhaps for others of more hospitable spirit what we have explored in this brief book will embolden them to consider and perhaps to embrace their immortal destiny.

Title: *Louisiana Rogue*
- Author: Harold Raley
- Publisher: Lamar University Press
- Paper Back: ISBN: 9780985255275
- eBook: Kindle
- Pages 306
- Publication Date: April 2013

This wonderfully entertaining picaresque novel by Harold Raley falls in the tradition of rogue literature established by Tom Jones and other early novels. Set in the nineteenth century, Louisiana Rogue will take you on a wild, fast-paced romp through all levels of Cajun society in the 1830s. The title page says the book promises to tell "The Life and Times of Pierre Prospère-Tourmoulin, Picket-pocket, Thief, Gambler, Fugitive, Undertaker, Barber, Doctor, Priest, Prisoner, Bandit, and Count; Latterly penned in his hand for the gentle reader of leisure, Spanning the years 1831-1839" and claims to be translated by his grandson, also named Peter Tourmoulin.

Title: *The Spirit of Spain*
- Author: Harold Raley
- Publisher: Halcyon Pr Ltd
- Paper Back: ISBN: 9780970605498
- Pages 212
- Publication Date: October, 2011

The Spirit of Spain brims with aperçus and revelations, many of them controversial, others startling, all engrossing. From Roman Hispania to the most recent Spanish trends, Professor Raley narrates the unique story of Spanish civilization. Examples of his original thinking include a "phenomenology of Spanish history," a new theory of the Spanish Renaissance, new concepts of Spanish patriotism and nationalism, and a reinterpretation of Spanish "Stoicism." As the book unfolds he also takes many sidelong looks into Hispanic America and offers a new explanation of Spain's relationship to Moslem Al-Andalus and modern Europe. The book culminates in a radical analysis of "Quixotic life" and its unsuspected significance for the post-modern age.

Title: *The Light of Eden:*
A Christian Worldview
- Author: Harold Raley
- Publisher: John M. Hardy Publishing
- Paper Back: ISBN: 9780979839122
- Pages 196
- Publication Date: May 2008

An inspiring vision of richer Christian life and thought. In the tradition of C. S. Lewis and G. K. Chesterton, this extraordinary book is both a spiritual adventure and an intellectual feast. Packed with illuminating insights and written in beautiful language, The Light of Eden introduces its readers to a vast treasury of creative ideas, innovative concepts, and possibilities contained in Christianity.

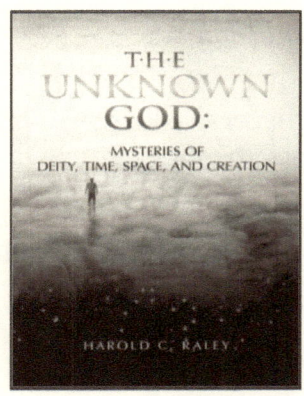

Title: *The Unknown God: Mysteries of Deity, Time, Space, and Creation*
- Author: Harold Raley
- Publisher: CreateSpace
- Paper Back: ISBN: 9781466273184
- Pages 142
- Publication Date: October, 2011

In his powerful Introduction to The Unknown God, religious thinker and writer Harold Raley makes this unusual request of the reader: "Suspend, if you will, everything you know about God. Put aside for the duration of this reading your traditional theologies and hear a new and more reverent way of thinking about God. When you return to your old understandings, they will have deeper meanings, unless those you once professed were meaningless to start with. If you are unwilling or unable to do as I ask, read no further. This message is not for you. The truth it contains will find you later when it is ready for you and you have been made ready for it." To approach Deity from this radically new perspective--arguably the greatest advance in theological thought of modern times--is to expose and shed light on the baffling paradoxes, improbable notions, and misleading errors not only about God but also about time, space, creation, and immortality. In each of these categories this book offers stunning new insights that incorporate not only the efforts of classical theologians but also the latest discoveries in science. Outline in these advanced insights is a new understanding of human life. By the law of corresponding identities, Raley explains, a more elevated theory of God necessarily means a more elevated theory of mankind. Each of the many themes and aperçus packed into this slender volume could have been a hefty tome. With pristine eloquence Raley reduces them to the essentials, believing as he does that clarity of style is courtesy to the reader.

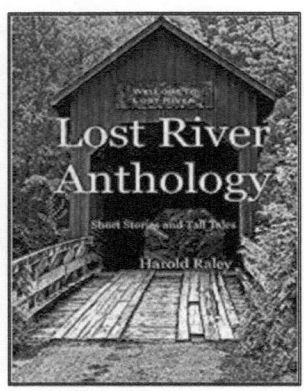

Title: *Lost River Anthology*
- Author: Harold Raley
- Publisher: Lamar University Press
- Paper Back: ISBN: 9781942956372
- Pages 212
- Publication Date: 2017

Internationally known writer and educator Harold Raley was born in Alabama and has lived and taught most of this life in the South and Southwest. His mastery of several languages and cultures, travels, and studies in a variety of disciplines has widened his perspective and enriched his literary technique but without weakening his allegiance to the rural times, myths, and people he loved first and best. They live again in Lost River Anthology as Raley elevates his craft to its finest pitch, composing a compelling melody of human drama and dignity cadenced by pathos, pain, love, humor, and salvific hope. The register covers a vast space of intertwined times and personalities, but always centered on the preeminent, unifying theme of human worth.

Title: *A Watch Over Mortality: The Philosophical Story of Julian Marias (SUNY series in Latin American and Iberian Thought and Culture)*
- Author: Harold Raley
- Publisher: SUNY Press;
- Paper Back: ISBN: 9780791431542
- Pages 289
- Publication Date: 1996

An in-depth study of the thought of contemporary Spanish philosopher Julian Marias, in the context of Ortega y Gasset and his times and twentieth-century Spanish culture.

In this book, Harold Raley offers the English-speaking world Julian Marias's compelling alternatives to contemporary minimalist thoughts, and does so in a dynamic style that itself reflects the humane spirit and verve of what may well prove to be the most innovative philosophy of modern times.

Title: *Adventures in Language*
Facts and Fictions of English
and Other Languages
- Author: Harold Raley
- Publisher: TotalRecall Publications;
- Paper Back: ISBN: 9781590955321
- Pages 216
- Publication Date: 2017

Even though at times I point out obvious errors in the languages as they are currently structured, I realize that the rules of grammar and usage in English or any other living language are, or can be, subject to change. This may not be true of, say, ancient Sanskrit, but then we note that despite its perfection—or perhaps because of it—ancient Sanskrit ceased to be a spoken tongue many centuries ago.

Over the ages thinkers have pondered the qualities that define humanity and set mankind apart from other species. In my view, no stronger case than language can be made for human uniqueness. Animals can communicate and mimic but they cannot speak. Language, sung, recited, or spoken, is archly human, and for that reason also deeply mysterious, beautiful, and fascinating.

Title: *Points of Light*
The Art of Being Human
- Author: Harold Raley
- Publisher: TotalRecall Publications;
- Paper Back: ISBN: 9781590955369
- Pages 240
- Publication Date: 2017

The real challenge for me, used as I was to academic and fiction writing, was the necessary brevity of the essays. The discipline of having to compress my ideas into a finite word count troubled me at first. Later, however, I was grateful for the experience because it forced me to get to the point and stay strictly on task. Instead of grumbling, I came to relish the challenge and to appreciate journalistic brevity as a special literary form more fitting for our hurried times than the ponderous writings of earlier, more leisurely times.

The themes treated are an entirely different matter. They are far-ranging, and the freedom I surrendered in linguistic spaciousness I gained back in the latitude I had to treat many topics as fairly and clearly in space permitted.

But there is method in what may appear to be unrelated themes. At a near or far remove, and from a variety of perspectives, all rest on the master concepts that undergird all my philosophical work: the uniqueness of human reality, the dignity, humor, and pathos of the person, and the possibilities of life that set it far apart and high above all other earthly realities.

Title: *Barefoot On A Frosty Morn*
- Author: Harold Raley
- Publisher: Mouse Gate Press
- Paper Back: ISBN: 9781590953426
- eBook ISBN: 9781590953433
- Pages 352
- Publication Date: October, 2016

Barefoot on a Frosty Morn is a literary and genealogical tapestry of several families over three centuries. The genealogical threads stretch back to England and France and unfold in step with America's continental expansion. The families crisscross north, south, and west as the tapestry grows in richness and complexity. A final episode sheds light on the earliest roots of the story. The reader has a perspective only partially available to the personalities immersed in the stories. Episodes are woven around some American milestones: the Revolution, the Civil War and WWII. These resonate and enrich but do not hinder the genealogical flow of the novel. In its conception and execution *Barefoot on a Frosty Morn* is unlike any writing before it. It surpasses the limits of history and narrates the essence of the American vision of life.

Title: *The Prodigal*
- Author: Harold Raley
- Publisher: Mouse Gate Press
- Paper Back: ISBN: 9781590953402
- eBook ISBN: 9781590953419
- Pages 96
- Publication Date: October, 2016

In the tradition of Crusoe and Sabatini, The Prodigal is a story of the shipwreck and struggle for survival of a young ship's carpenter who escapes one captivity only to fall into more dangerous circumstances. The story unfolds from Boston to Mexico, Cuba, Africa, and back again. At critical points a mysterious stranger intervenes to lend a hand and guide him to his destiny.